Poiema

New and Selected Poems

Poiema

New and Selected Poems

Cherie Burbach

Poiema: New and Selected Poems

Poiema
New and Selected Poems

Bonjour Publishing

All rights reserved.

Copyright © 2018 by Cherie Burbach

POIEMA: NEW AND SELECTED POEMS

All rights reserved. No part of this book may be reproduced by mechanical, photographic, or electronic process, or in the form of a photographic recording; nor may it be stored in a retrieval system, transmitted, or otherwise be copied for public or private use - other than for "fair use" as brief quotations embodied in articles and reviews without prior written permission of the publisher.

Printed in the United States of America

For
my husband

Also by Cherie Burbach

Nonfiction

Art and Faith: Mixed Media Art With a Faith-Filled Message
Prayer Warrior Journal
100 Simple Ways to Have More Friends
Glass Sculptures: How to Make Beautiful Sculptures for the Garden Using Vases, Bowls, and Other Glass Pieces
...and more

Poetry

Angel Toughness
My Soul Is From a Different Place
Father's Eyes
The Difference Now
A New Dish
New and Selected Poems
Yes, You

The Poems

New and Previously Unpublished Poems 1990-2018

Truth
Women's March
If Dogs Could Talk
The Light of the Beloved
Breath of Life
God Speaks
Gracefully Dancing
Faith
Home
Princess
Thank You
Roberta
Seasons of Life and Big Girl Tears
Children of the World
Tree Girl
Our Beauty
Some Children
I Once Believed
Hope
Silence
Red-Tailed Hawk and Gray Wolf
This Is the Moment
Your Pretty Words
The Blessing of Genevieve
Can You Erase Years
Little Girl's Soul
The Thing I Don't Appreciate Enough
Poiema
His Amazing Love
Be Still and Know

Maple Tree
My Angel Dog
Never Lost
He Loves You
Perfect
Mystery Path
Sweet Friend

Angel Toughness
2015

All Right
New Path
Blaming the Sun
Loved by the Creator
Granny
Beware the Lion
Dear Younger Self
Angel Toughness
Hope
A Little Slice of Heaven
Birthday Prayer
My Heart
Glorious Day
Silent Hummingbird
The Grace of a New Day
Where Evening Fades (Tangerine Clouds)
Hummingbird
God's Currency
End of Day (Rest, Happy)

My Soul Is From a Different Place
2014

Kiss That Scar
The Purpose of Pain
Our Beautiful Brokenness
The Basket
You Should Know
Each Time You Smile
Simple Kindness
This House Had
Finite
Robin's Nest
Early Morning Choir
What Is Prayer?
Free Pass
Afternoon Cinema
The Smile
Cardinal
My Soul Is From a Different Place
A Cloak of Forgiveness
This Is What I Crave
Every Jagged Edge
Called
The Blessing In My Sleepless Night
Beacon
High Regard

Cherie Burbach

Yes, You
2012

Yes, You
Rise Above That Past So Dark
Filled With Your Spirit
Dear Women
The Cost of Addiction
Family Nap
The Suicides
I Send Out My Prayers
The Mentor
The Clear Blue Sky
My Prayers
Soar
Forever Yours
Inspired by Grace
Shine
Homesick
You Count My Tears

New and Selected Poems
2011

Waiting Expectantly
The Story of Me
Silently I Read Mary Oliver's Poetry
Awake
Up
By Poetry
The Wise Bride
Do You Love Me?
Happily Ever After
Spring
Perfect Love
No Power Here
In the Blink of an Eye
It's Your Answer
Salt of the Ocean

Father's Eyes
2007

What I Didn't Know
His Child
Strength, I Yearn
Survive

Cherie Burbach

A New Dish
2005

Go The Right Way
Words
Cast Away Lilies
On Trial
Jagged Rocks
This Is Who I Am
A Step or Two Behind
With Tired Eyes
Yes
Father's Eyes
Our New Home
Take My Hand
Worry
Fallen Short
How Will I Find You Again?
Is That All There Is
Marriage
Before I Need To Ask
This Man I Love
Bouquet Wrapped With Trust
Keep Going, Child
This Night

The Difference Now
2004

The Girl You Drew On Canvas
Your Life, My Lesson
I Am
There Goes The Girl
To Face The Mighty Thunder
It Started With a Word
How Far
Behind My Smile
Most Times
This House
If Life Were a Book
Deepest Void
Today, I Take For Me
Tomorrow, She Walks With Grace
Like Old Men in Rocking Chairs
Read the Label
Real Life Princess
Forgive
I'm Not That Girl
Angel In Waiting
Could It Be
I Could Make Believe
At The Coffee Shop
The Difference Now
Tell Me Again
With Every Breath

Intro

Thank you for purchasing *Poiema*.

It's interesting how a Bible verse you've heard many times can suddenly have new meaning. A few years ago someone posted the words from Ephesians 2:10 and included the Greek translation. The King James Version of this verse is:

"For we are his workmanship, created in Christ Jesus unto good works, which God hath before ordained that we should walk in them."

The Greek word Paul chose for "workmanship" was "poiema," which is where we get the modern word "poem."

We are God's poem.

In viewing the verse using this context, I felt a chill. Poetry has always been special to me. I have used it as a way to express myself and comfort myself as a child.

I always wrote short stories and painted as a kid, but when I was eight my second grade teacher told me I had a "poetic way of writing" and I should try writing poetry. She didn't teach me anything about poetry, however. She didn't point out any poems I should study. She just told me I should write it and moved on.

This moment stands out for me because of how small and simple it seemed at the time. Now, looking back, I see that this was a profound moment of grace working in my life.

My second grade teacher probably had no idea of how much this suggestion would help me. Ironically, I was sure this teacher didn't like me. She didn't sit with me and teach me things individually as my other teachers had up until that point. I didn't realize it until later, but I had been spoiled by other teachers. They recognized me as "gifted" so when I finished my work I got to go off to a little corner by myself, where I was happiest. I was an introvert, and school was often too much for me: too loud, too many voices, too many images. I got my work done quickly and then I was bored.

My first grade teacher would let me go off to a corner of the classroom, (supplied with unlimited amounts of paper and paint, which was heaven to a kid like me) and there I would write and paint and create. Then, she'd take the stories or drawings I had created and present them to class. I was equal parts embarrassed and thrilled at this.

After second grade, I would go to class in the mornings, get my assignments, and then do everything from stock shelves to run messages around the school in the afternoons. I'd come back just before school was over, get my homework assignments, and then go home. I liked this arrangement. My introverted self was comfortable being alone, so working in the library, which was not only quiet but surrounded by books, was the perfect place for me.

But my second grade teacher, who was one of the few who refused to give me busy work in this way, gave me instead the greatest gift of all: a suggestion that I could write poetry. The first couple times I tried it, I wrote what I thought a poem was supposed to be, and I remember trying very hard to rhyme. I had lines like *I walk around the house as quiet as a mouse…*

My first couple attempts were impersonal and terrible. I wish I still had them. But even then, I had developed the habit of writing as if my life depended on it at night and then ripping up my poetry in the morning. The act of writing in those days is what blessed me the most. I worked through issues and figured out the world this way, and the melodic nature of poetry (rhymed or not) helped to calm me, making me feel safe enough to sleep.

Something ignited in me in those early attempts at poetry. My poems quickly changed from being what I thought a poem was supposed to be to what I wanted to express. And back then, I had a lot of emotions to tap from.

I was given away for adoption, then raised in an alcoholic household where I dealt with many different types of abuse. I was an unhappy kid, confused about my life and what God wanted from me. I was told I was worthless and unwanted, and as an only child, I spent much of the time alone.

But I always had creativity. I could express the anger or hurt or sadness I felt through my short stories and paintings, and when the suggestion of writing poetry was floated my way I grasped it like a passing life raft.

I continued writing poetry throughout my teens and 20s, but most of it wound up in the garbage. Then, when I was 30 years old, my father lost his battle with alcoholism and ended his life. I grieved his death but there was also a sense of relief that my tormentor was gone. For the first time, I started keeping my poetry. Five years later, I started working on my first poetry book, *The Difference Now*. I went on to publish a few more books, become a full-time writer, and then eventually, a full-time artist.

And then I saw Ephesians 2:10 posted with the Greek translation for workmanship, and felt almost as if God was speaking directly to me: *we are His poiema*. We weren't just another one of his creations, we were so special we were *His poem*. I've been thinking about this ever since and knew that for this newest poetry book I wanted to do a retrospective of sorts that tells the story of what being His poiema is really like.

My story has had many ups and downs, but I recognize God's blessings at work in my life. It took me years to develop a healthy view of His love because for many years, I felt that because bad things happened to me God just didn't like me. I had many traumas early on and when I got older I sabotaged good things in my life because I felt that I didn't deserve them. I felt constantly unworthy of love, and my life choices reflected that.

But God is the best teacher! He has worked me through all that, pulled me through, and patiently and lovingly taught me that being His child is all I need. Looking back through the dark years, I saw His hand at work in my life and realized He had been there all along.

I think it is important that in seeing ourselves as His poiema, we have to see the blessing in everything. This is a hard concept. When you're struggling, it is difficult to thank God and see Him still there working for your good. But He is. I know this now. Even though the dark years are behind me my life is still full of both hardships and great blessings. Yours probably is, too. I have pondered my life and wondered what it would have been like without the childhood trauma, but looking at things that way gives an incomplete picture. I am the person I am because of every moment before. You, too. So don't wish away the past. Accept that wherever you have been, God was there, too. You might not understand the reason things happened or didn't happen. Some things are just too profound for our minds and hearts, and only God knows the complete picture.

You can forgive the past without having the anger and hurt follow you around and prevent you from embracing all the good you were meant to have. Forgiving the past sometimes means you are able to have relationships with the ones who hurt you, sometimes it means you need healthy boundaries with them, and sometimes it means loving them from a distance without them actively in your life. Only you know what's right, and believe me, people will tell you their opinions. But the only way to make the right decision is to pray and ask God, then listen to the answer. Forget what people say and suggest. They love to tell you how to live, but their suggestions are based on their own experience, on their own hurt and happiness and desires. God will tell you what's right, but you have to get past the noise of society and social media and even well-meaning people who love you in order to hear what God is trying to say.

God cares about you and every small detail in your life. In the human life we don't have the luxury of being without conflict or struggle. That's what heaven is for. But we can see the purpose in our lives, and acknowledge the gift of being God's poiema.

Table of Contents

The Poems 11

Intro 19

Table of Contents 25

Chapter 1: 35

The Blessing in Struggle 35

    Kiss That Scar.. 37

    The Purpose of Pain 39

    The Girl You Drew On Canvas 41

    Your Life, My Lesson 43

    I Am... 44

    There Goes The Girl.. 45

    To Face The Mighty Thunder....................................... 46

    It Started With a Word.. 47

    How Far... 50

    Go The Right Way.. 51

    Strength, I Yearn... 52

    Salt of the Ocean 53

    Words... 54

    Can You Erase Years... 55

    Behind My Smile... 56

    Cast Away Lilies 57

    Most Times 58

Survive *60*
You Count My Tears *61*
Perfect *63*
On Trial *64*
This House *65*
If Life Were a Book *67*
Deepest Void *68*
Today, I Take For Me *70*
Tomorrow, She Walks With Grace *72*
Like Old Men in Rocking Chairs *74*
Read the Label *75*
Real Life Princess *78*
Little Girl's Soul *81*
A Step or Two Behind *83*
This Is Who I Am *85*
With Tired Eyes *86*
Yes *87*
Waiting Expectantly *88*
The Story of Me *90*
Silently I Read Mary Oliver's Poetry *93*
Never Lost *95*
Home *98*
Awake *99*
Up *100*
By Poetry *102*
The Wise Bride *103*

Hope 105
Forgive 108
All Right 109
New Path 111
Blaming the Sun 113
Roberta 114
I'm Not That Girl 117
Father's Eyes 118
Our Beautiful Brokenness 120

Chapter 2: 125
Embracing His Divine Purpose 125

Yes, You 127
Our New Home 129
What I Didn't Know 132
Take My Hand 134
Angel In Waiting 136
Seasons of Life and Big Girl Tears 139
Rise Above That Past So Dark 142
The Basket 143
Worry 147
Fallen Short 149
How Will I Find You Again? 151
You Should Know 152
Is That All There Is 153
Do You Love Me? 155

Happily Ever After *157*
Filled With Your Spirit *158*
Each Time You Smile *159*
Marriage *160*
Dear Women *161*
The Cost of Addiction *162*
Family Nap *163*
The Suicides *165*
I Send Out My Prayers *168*
The Mentor *170*
Princess *171*
Simple Kindness *172*
This House Had *174*
Loved by the Creator *176*
Granny *178*
Truth *180*
Breath of Life *181*
Women's March *182*
Children of the World *184*
Tree Girl *188*
Our Beauty *191*
Some Children *193*
I Once Believed *194*
Silence *195*
Red-Tailed Hawk and Gray Wolf *196*
This Is the Moment *202*

Could It Be 203
Perfect Love 204
I Could Make Believe 205
Spring 206
At The Coffee Shop 207
The Difference Now 208
Tell Me Again 210
This Man I Love 211
Sweet Friend 212
Bouquet Wrapped With Trust 213
No Power Here 215
Finite 216
Beware the Lion 217
Your Pretty Words 219
In the Blink of an Eye 222
Dear Younger Self 223

Chapter 3: **225**
How Manifold Are His Works **225**
Angel Toughness 227
Gracefully Dancing 229
Robin's Nest 230
Early Morning Choir 233
The Clear Blue Sky 234
The Blessing of Genevieve 235
What Is Prayer? 236

Free Pass *238*

Hope *240*

Afternoon Cinema *241*

The Smile *242*

Cardinal *243*

A Little Slice of Heaven *244*

Birthday Prayer *247*

My Heart *249*

Glorious Day *251*

Silent Hummingbird *252*

God Speaks *253*

The Light of the Beloved *254*

If Dogs Could Talk *256*

The Thing I Don't Appreciate Enough *257*

Poiema *259*

My Angel Dog *260*

Maple Tree *262*

The Grace of a New Day *264*

Where Evening Fades (Tangerine Clouds) *265*

Hummingbird *267*

Chapter 4: 269

Gifts of His Grace 269

My Soul Is From a Different Place *271*

Keep Going, Child *272*

With Every Breath *273*

You Have Seen Us Through 275
This Night 278
It's Your Answer 279
My Prayers 281
Soar 282
Forever Yours 284
Inspired by Grace 286
Shine 288
A Cloak of Forgiveness 289
This Is What I Crave 292
Every Jagged Edge 293
Called 296
The Blessing In My Sleepless Night 297
Beacon 299
God's Currency 301
End of Day (Rest, Happy) 303
Mystery Path 304
Faith 306
His Amazing Love 307
Be Still and Know 309
High Regard 310
He Loves You 312
Homesick 313
His Child 314

About the Author **319**

Poiema: New and Selected Poems

Chapter 1:

The Blessing in Struggle

Kiss That Scar

Kiss that scar
the one that is jagged, and rough,
the one that you try and hide
because you think that it is ugly.

Rub your palm lovingly
across the hard edges
of its surface,
embrace the design of that scar,
chosen especially for you
by God.

To think only of the pain
when you see that scar
is to forget who you are:
beautiful
strong
filled with compassion
filled with purpose.

The scar does not represent
what you lost,
it shows you all that you gained,
all that you could never
have purchased
with all the riches of the world.

The scar is your awakening,
to you, and everyone who
crosses your path.
It says pay attention,
God showed me where
my heart had been buried.

Kiss that scar
and feel the message,
written out in code,
that only you can decipher.
A secret, shared by God's whisper
into your entire soul,
then spread out into the world
with every beat of your heart.

The Purpose of Pain

How do you know
that this pain you feel
is darkness tugging
at your soul?

How do you know
that the hurt
is an attack
from your enemies?

Perhaps the pain
is from angels feverishly
sewing thousands of stitches
deep into your spine.

Each stitch meant
to hold wings
firmly in place
for eternity.

And when you stretch
your arms up above your head
the pain becomes almost unbearable.
Almost.

But you get used to the feeling
and mistakenly believe
it's because pain
is your legacy in life.

When really your soul
is finally learning to adjust
to the power
of its reach.

And when you stretch
your arms again
as wide as they can go,
you can finally embrace God.

The Girl You Drew On Canvas

I took your lies
      like a bouquet of roses.
I told you they smelled beautiful
      and put them in a vase, with water
      so they stayed fresh.

I accepted your insults
      like a handmade sweater.
I slipped them over my head
      and pressed the fabric into my skin
      making sure it covered every inch.

I bathed in your cold stares
      running the water over my body.
Until I convinced myself it was warm enough
      and I'd sink deep down
      until I was soaked.

I played your criticism
      like a jazz CD.
I poured a glass of wine
      and listened while the melodies
      washed over me.

I saw your sketch of me
      and took in every angle.
I stared at the painting
      until I could see the girl
      you drew on canvas.

I opened my arms
        and embraced your arrogance.
I held it close to my heart
        like a gift of true love
            sent from above.

Your Life, My Lesson

From the depths of madness
which beckoned his soul,

to the echoes of sadness
which swallow me whole,

so lies the demons
who laugh at my life,

so lies the fate
of my father and I.

I move on without you
forever I mourn,

your hatred has scarred me
but my life is reborn.

I Am

I am the guilt of my father's illness
I am the burden of his death
I am evidence of his addiction.

I am
        every word in my childhood diary
        like a moment of history
            written long ago
        or a far away fable
        truth recorded in black and white
        to be read on a Sunday morning
        coolly now, dispassionately
        telling the tale
            of the child he chose to ignore
            and the woman he refused to see

I am his every success and failure.

There Goes The Girl

There goes the girl
who'd inherit the world,
there goes the girl
with the smile.

Some look at the girl
then look past her world
to see only her life
without trial.

So this strong little girl
begs you into her world
can you see her true self
for a while?

The arms of this girl
held out for the world
remain empty, save for
loneliness, stretching for miles.

And the tears of this girl
wash her life from this world
while you admire the view
from her isle.

Cherie Burbach

To Face The Mighty Thunder

I spat a word today
that floated through the air.
It cursed my faith away
and made me stop and stare.

When did this life of mine
get lost among the years.
Where friends upon a time
now leave me to my tears.

I wander all alone
without a map or guide.
The highest flights I've flown
then crash down upon my pride.

How many times, I wonder
must this shy girl begin again?
And face the mighty thunder
holding only a single pen.

It Started With a Word

It started with a word
from a father to a son.
Why can't you be more like me,
he said.
For my pride you are not the one.

The boy's heart filled up with sadness.
Then the sadness turned to rage.
Why can't I be smart and strong,
he said, like other boys my age.

The boy read every book and volume,
but inside, he remained the same.
I can't become this man, he thought,
that for my father causes shame.

I will grow up strong,
he thought at last,
and be a man that others fear.
My father will see how others run
and with his pride will cheer.

The son's eyes grew wide with power
while his heart grew cold as stone.
He developed a strong army
and with them, never felt alone.

They terrorized the hills and soon,
they started a little war.
This must be love, he thought at last,
then killed a little more.

He waited for his father's smile
he waited for his pride.
He hoped to hear those words of love,
to heal his emptiness inside.

Instead his father hid in shame.
How could this be my son?
What did I do that was so wrong,
I loved him, my only one.

With pain still deep within his soul
the son decided what to do,
he'd start a family of his own,
with his son, he'd begin anew.

He found a wife, then pressured her,
to have a baby boy.
On the day his son was finally born
his heart filled up with joy.

The years grew on, his son grew tall,
but his father was unimpressed.
If this son deserves my name,
then he must be the very best.

He must be stronger, tougher
than I see him now to be.
He must become a man, he thought,
he must be more like me.

The boy listened, and, with heavy heart,
decided what to do.
I must be tougher, stronger
Oh father, I must be more like you!

He climbed a tree, while his father watched
and wrung the neck of a tiny bird.
The pattern started once again,
and it started with a word.

How Far

How far the distance
      between the heart and the mind?
How far to erase
      those words so unkind?

How far must I stand
      before the mirror and stare,
      until the ugliness fades,
      until the beauty is there.

Is there a place I can find
      where your words have not spread?
Is there a place in this world
      where I won't hear what you've said?

How far is this distance?
How far must I go?
To think you were wrong
and tell my heart it is so.

Go The Right Way

Driver
        please take me back
        to where I first went wrong
        so I can correct my path
        and go the right way.

There's
        a placed called Childhood.
        Can you take me back there?
        I believe that's where
        I took a wrong turn
        and I could start again
        I could change my way.

Driver
        what's the fare
        to take me back in time?
        How much do I owe
        for such a trip?

I'd
        have to pay you
        all my wisdom?
        And there's no guarantee
        I'd find my way
        on a different path?

Let's
        go 'round the block again
        and when I emerge from this ride
        perhaps I'll get my bearings
        and see that I was heading
        the right way, all along.

Cherie Burbach

Strength, I Yearn

I walked away,
        but you didn't follow.
I turned to stay,
        but instead felt hollow.

I had to leave.
        I could not stay.
But did you grieve
        for love today?

I left this life
        with quiet sleep.
Laid down with strife
        and strong beliefs.

Strength, I yearn.
        Erase the pain.
I won't return.
        Begin again.

Salt of the Ocean

If I had a net
and could catch your words
I'd stuff them in a bottle
and let them drift into the deep blue ocean.

And the kind words
would float to the top
like weightless air
like a gentle breeze.

And the cruel words
would mix with the salt in the ocean
and the salt of broken-hearted tears
and sink to the bottom.

And I would take my net
and capture each kind word
and bring them back into our world
so we could start over.

Words

Words thrown up to heaven
      desperate pleas of fate.
Words relaying sorrow
      a life succumb to hate.

Words that lead aggression
      pulling anger from the beast.
Words that beg forgiveness
      a melancholy feast.

Words that fight my smile
      taunting from inside.
Words with caged aggression
      fearful of the ride.

Words with charmed benevolence
      beckoning me near.
Words spat with poison venom
      now all I seem to hear.

Can You Erase Years

Can you erase years
> but leave what I've learned?

Can you take me back
> to the turn I missed?

Can you change me back
> to the girl that believed promises?

Can you restore my faith
> and give me reasons to hope?

Can you show me the girl
> who dreamed of a different life?

Can you erase years
> but leave what I've learned?

Behind My Smile

I tried to find you
little one
with innocence
and songs begun.

I searched for you
through aging eyes
with memories
of sad good-byes.

Some said that you
could never die
so I searched my soul
to ask you why.

I longed for you
when sadness rained
I prayed for you
while sorrow gained.

Oh tell me now
my oldest friend
will hope return
will anger end?

And will I find you
behind my smile
and will you leave
or stay awhile?

Cast Away Lilies

I sent away my dreams today,
and set them on a paper boat
so they could sail across the ocean.

They'd stayed with me so long,
they weren't sure
where to go at first.

They asked if they could stay awhile,
floating on the water
like cast away lilies.

But they deserved better than my neglect,
so I gently blew on the sails
casting them out into the open.

I felt a chill with the wind that came to take them away
and wondered if I'd see them again
or if they'd one day drift back my way.

Most Times

I rush through my life
    every second planned
    every minute scheduled
    never saying no
    keeping up the game.

That's what you'll see,
    most times.

But most times
    I'm exhausted
    pushing my body
    harder, faster
    wondering how I can get up tomorrow
    and start the whole thing again.

That's how I feel,
    most times.

And most times,
    when I fall in bed at night
    knowing it is already too late
    for me to sleep
    waiting
    to close my eyes and dream.

Most times
    I can't even tell
    that my bed is empty
    as I lay by the side
    of dreams deferred
    and slip under the cover of loneliness.

Most times
>   I can't slow down
>   long enough
>   to see if this life
>   I fight for each day
>   is the one that I really want.

Most times
>   I just keep going
>   and pray that my destiny
>   will ride up one day
>   and tell me I've waited long enough
>   and I can finally slow down, and live.

That's what keeps me going,
>   most times.

Survive

The father who abused me
the managers who used me
the everyman who pushed me down,
you taught me to survive.

The men who slapped my face
and brought me to disgrace
to all of those who wished me harm,
you taught me to survive.

The boys who laughed and taunted
and those whose evil haunted
to all the bullies of this world,
you taught me to survive.

To those who think you'll bring me down
and try to turn my world around
to all of you, in spite of you,
I'm determined to survive.

You Count My Tears

You count my tears
as individual victories
falling one by one
as your self-importance grows.

You count my tears
as musical notes
that sing you to sleep at night.

You count my tears
as proof that I am
too emotional
too weak
too sensitive
too immature
too unpolished
while you congratulate yourself
on your composure.

You count my tears
as proof that
your words matter.
They have made an impact
and thus
you must be right.

You count my tears
as each drop becomes a rhythm
that you dance to,
swaying side to side,
eyes closed,
head tilted toward the sky,
as if to say
look at me, Lord!
See how good I am.

Perfect

Pretending an
Extraordinary
Reality
Forms her
Existence, while
Crying
To herself.

Cherie Burbach

On Trial

In some ways I'm an old woman
with a lifetime of memories past.
And sometimes I'm a child
with a smile that will always last.

But the person I've become
is not who I wanted to be.
And I wish I could tell you this anger
is not really a part of me.

So I do my best to get through each day
and to you, I present this smile.
Then I lie in bed, alone each night,
and put my life on trial.

This House

I am back in this house
        again.
Back in the room
        that I ran to,
        and hid in.

Back to the room
        that I cried in,
        while I tried to understand you.

Back in the room
        where I laid my head
        filled with self-doubt,
        and tried to sleep.

But sleep would taunt me
        not only in this house,
        but in any house I would live in.

Your words
        would penetrate my brain
        and soon
        become my conscience.

And this house
        became my prison.
This room,
        my cell.

And this house,
        became a place of fear.

I walked around this house
    keeping your secret.
And soon,
    I would not know you at all.

Soon...
    you would be gone.
        Leaving questions...
    leaving answers.

Soon...
    you would leave this house.

And I would hesitate
    to come back,
    because I knew that I would cry,
    and once again be filled with fear.

But this time...
    it would be different.
This time...
    my tears would carry me
    to a river of salvation.

And the anger... and the violence
    would be washed away
    by the love of my family
    by the kindness of my friends.

And so I come back
    to this house
    and I will not leave
        until it is filled with goodness and love
        and the spirit of God.

Until this house
    becomes a home.

If Life Were a Book

If life were a book,
> and we could read ahead
> to find out the ending,

> the pages in between
> would surely be filled with
> kind words, love, and honesty.

But
> instead we live day by day
> reflecting back on the things we've done,
> and, sometimes,
> wondering why we did them.

Instead of realizing
> that we do have the power
> to write our own life's story,
> to control our own destiny,
> we let life lead us around.

And we follow...
> hoping that eventually we'll end up
> with a happy ending.

Cherie Burbach

Deepest Void

When I was young, I prayed for you
and in the place near my heart
I carved a hole to fill with understanding.

As years grew on, you'd yell and cry and threaten
and in that hole I placed fear
and prayed for compassion.

Time went on, I saw your way
I saw myself through your eyes
and in that hole I placed self-loathing.

As the elements of fear and hatred grew
the hole I carved became bigger
until it could house self-sabotage, depression, and anger.

This hole became so large
I wondered for a time if it was really my soul
so I let it grow as large as it wanted to be.

Then came a day, when anger became tired
and even though it left that hole
the deepest void remained.

Understanding took up more space
and allowed forgiveness to stay by its side
self-loathing remained, but grew smaller.

On the day you left, tears flowed over me
and washed away doubts and confusion
but the hole remained, and made room for regret.

Today, I fill that hole with prayer,
and with love from friends and family.
I do not try to close the hole, I leave it open.

If self-loathing wishes to remain
it knows now it is not welcome.
If anger comes to visit
I let prayer transform it into forgiveness.

I let prayer rule the emptiness inside of me,
and I let go, and pray that God will fill
this deepest void
with love from others,
      for others,
           for myself.

Today, I Take For Me

Today
      I will look in the mirror
      for the little girl I left behind,
      and I will ask her to show me
           how to giggle, again.

Today
      I will talk to God,
      and I will not ask Him
      for a better job, a better house,
           a better life....

Today
      I will thank Him.
      Sincerely thank Him
      for giving me this interesting life,
      filled with surprises
           and the ability to laugh.

Today
      I will let the phone ring
      because those who are my friends
      will understand,
      and those who aren't,
           well...

Today
      I take for me.

Today
    I will let Cather calm my mind,
    and Shakespeare ease my soul,
    and Hamilton, Lipman, Kingsolver and Buck
        awe me with their talent.

Today
    I will acknowledge my own talent.

Today
    I will watch the snow
    fall down outside
    and see how it gives the world
    a fresh start
    making things clean again
        with its fresh blanket of white.

Today
    I will curl up in my favorite chair,
    and hug my curves and smile,
    and realize my best asset
        is my uniqueness.

Today
    I take for me.

Tomorrow, She Walks With Grace

Tomorrow…
    I will be a new woman.
    I will smile like a girl with thin thighs.

    I will close my eyes and breathe deeply
    exhaling bad thoughts from all the days before.

    I will remain silent
    listening to God
    greeting Him with a welcoming mind.

Tomorrow…
    I will get up early.

    I will be thankful for my ability to rise again.
        Like a warrior.
        Facing a new day.
        Strong.
        Ready.

Tomorrow…
    I will laugh like a child
        and wonder why adults don't play more.

Tomorrow…
  I will move my muscles.
    Drink cleansing water.
    Eat good food.
    Not drive so fast.
    Not be so angry.

Tomorrow…
  I will not think about the mistakes
    I made on any day before.
  I will walk with wisdom
    and know I have earned it.

Tomorrow…
  I will not hear the snickering,
    the laughter of those who claim to be friends.

I will move further down that road of understanding,
    climbing to the highest perch,
    so I can look out on all God offers.

Tomorrow…
  A new woman will emerge
    from this tired cocoon.
  She will no longer wish that same desire.
  She will understand her fate.
    Solitary in nature,
     with angels for companions.

Tomorrow…
  She will be the woman
  that walks with grace.

Cherie Burbach

Like Old Men in Rocking Chairs

Angry words
    framed the doorway
    of the house where I grew up.
And there was no way to enter
    without those words,
        tainted and searing,
        landing upon your soul.

They evaporated
    into your skin
    and you couldn't wash them away
    or cover them
        with the fragrance of kindness.

They embedded each cell
    of your heart and mind
        and shaped the person you saw
        when you looked into the mirror.
And the tears
    that tried to wash them away
    only made them grow.

And when I thought
    they had left me,
    they were really sitting in the corner
        like old men in rocking chairs
            watching, waiting,
            until happiness fades
                and they can say
                    I told you so.

Read the Label

You gave me a dress
> but it was too small.
> I looked at the label
> and it said "unfeeling and ungrateful."

When I told you it didn't quite fit
> you suggested I lose weight.
> I ate what you prepared
> and when the dress you bought me
>> still didn't fit,
>> I stopped eating.

Now the skirt slid over my hips
> but I still felt uncomfortable.
> I realized it was the wrong color and style.

You said
> since I was good
> and lost weight
> you'd buy me a new one.

But I couldn't go with you
> or make the choice myself.

You'd pick out my new clothes
> and if I didn't like them
> I could go entirely without.

The new skirt's label
> said "lazy and stupid."
> I didn't want to try it on
> but you made me.

And I didn't protest
> I didn't want to argue
> or give you the impression
> that I wasn't a nice girl.

So I put on the new skirt.
    It was short, and tight.
    You said it looked good
    that it fit me perfectly.
    So I tried to be happy
    and be what you wanted me to be.

You told me girls were quiet
    they didn't talk back.
    So I held my tongue
    even though I disagreed with you.
But then you told me I didn't talk enough
    that I was stupid
    and slow.

So I tried to show you I was smart.
    I had a mind of my own
    that I wanted to share.

But when I told you my dreams
    you shoved me down.
    You told me no one would ever want me
    and I would always be alone.
    And then you gave me a new skirt to wear.

This skirt's label read
    "difficult and unlovable."
    I put on my new skirt
    but cried softly in my room.
I wore that skirt for a long time
    even when I had outgrown it
    I still told myself that it fit.

Every once in a while
        someone would ask
        why I wore that skirt.
        They would tell me it didn't fit,
        and I should get a new one.
But I didn't want to upset you
        so I chased them away
                from my life.

But one day
        I walked past a store window
        and saw a beautiful blue skirt
        long and flowing.
I walked in the store
        and tried it on.

"It looks good on you,"
        the salesclerk said
        as I spun around in front of the mirror.
I felt good, real, beautiful.
I read the label,
        "passionate and honest."
"It really is you," the clerk said again.
        And for the first time
                I believed it.

"I'll take it," I said,
        and handed her the money.
"In fact," I said, "I'll wear it out of the store."

I handed the clerk my old skirt
        and told her I didn't want it anymore.
As I walked out
        I looked at the mirror one more time,
                and smiled.

Real Life Princess

For just one day
    of this life
        filled with challenges and hurdles and
        dreams

    let me be
    a princess…
        real life,
        house in the suburbs,
        2.5 kids
            princess.

Let me work
    not because I have to
    not because I need to bust it each day
    but because I need something to do.

Let my biggest complaint
    be that my husband works late
    and "doesn't help" with laundry.

Let me know
    what it feels like
    to share the burden of worries
    to cut off a slice and hand it to my partner
    when it gets overwhelming
        "Here Honey, why don't you take the
        last piece? I couldn't possibly stomach
        another bite."

Let me have lunch with friends
    leisurely
    not watching the clock
    not thinking about what I have to do
    back in the office.
Let me enjoy
    a cool glass of water
    with a twist of lemon
    a salad, low fat
    with vinaigrette.

Let that one person
    who hates everything about me
    be not the coworker out to sabotage my job
    but the blonde woman at PTA
    who hates me because I speak my mind.

Just for one day
    let me lay my head down
    next to a real life prince
        not perfect
        not wealthy
        not completing me
        not making me whole

    but there
        beside me
        with me
        sharing this life of
            happiness
            worry
            grief
            love

taking a burden from my arms
    like a bag of groceries
    not to keep forever
    but to take off my hands
        just long enough
        to let me rest my sore muscles
        so I can pick them back up
        and push on.

For just one day
    let me wake up in the life of a real life princess.

Let me turn down the pace of this life
    so I can finally hear what it is saying to me.

Little Girl's Soul

There is a little girl
with blue eyes
and a sad smile,

who has bags
under her eyes
from too many nights
watching her bedroom
door in fear.

Let us hold her,
and remove the
crown of shame
that should never have
been hers to wear.

Tell her
she is precious,
and innocent,

remind her
that God is there
for her,

and she should
cling to Him
each moment.

Help her pack up
her pride and faith
and leave the rest,

and follow the path
that God has laid
before her.

Picture herself
born anew,
with that
little girl's soul.

A Step or Two Behind

I saw you there
>your force made strong
>with my failures
>and past mistakes
>I saw you
>but left anyway
>when the sun rose up to mark a new day
>and shined brightly on the path ahead.

I walked fast
>aware of you, close on my heels
>whispering that you were here
>to take me back.
>I even stopped a time or two
>and entertained you for a night.
>But in the morning
>I left again
>running this time
>as fast and far as I could get
>with all my strength.

I ran so hard
>I sometimes forgot where I was going
>and I'd look over my shoulder
>to see you running along with me
>keeping pace all the way.
>Sometimes I'd stumble
>and you'd catch me,
>and for a short while,
>I felt something familiar.
>You told me it was love.

Cherie Burbach

I stayed with you then
        acquiescing to your force.
        It was easier than running;
        but when I held out my arms
        to fully embrace you,
        I found I had lots of room left
        to wrap them around
        something else.

I left again
        and I knew you'd follow.
        I didn't run
        but I kept walking
        I'd see you time and again
        a step or two behind,
        still there,
        but no longer wishing to catch up to me,
        and I'd nod, acknowledge you,
        then head off again.
        Everyone knows you're there,
        and I know I don't belong with you,
        so I move forward with each new day,
        until I find out where I do.

This Is Who I Am

This is who I am
a girl, a smile.
This is who I am
with simple style.

This is who I am
a saddened past.
This is who I am
content at last.

This is who I am
with body ill.
This is who I am
surviving still.

This is who I am
right now, this day.
This is who I am
in every way.

This is who I am
a spirit strong.
This is who I've been
all along.

Cherie Burbach

With Tired Eyes

With tired eyes
I see my past
with tired eyes
I plan.

Building on a million yesterdays
to now do all I can.

With tired eyes
I hike the hills
with tired eyes
I go.

Until I believe you were wrong about me
and my heart knows it is so.

With tired eyes
I'll chart my course
with tired eyes
I soar.

I'll work until I find that place
where the world will offer more.

With tired eyes
I'll look at you
with tired eyes
I'll see.

You can't tell me who I am
my world is defined by me.

Yes

Yes, I've got charisma.
Yes, I've got the might.
Yes, I will go on and I will not give up the fight.

Yes, you were mistaken.
Yes, you were quite wrong.
Yes, you have misjudged me with it all and for so long.

Yes, I ask forgiveness.
Yes, I kneel to pray.
Yes, I ask His guidance and His grace with every day.

Yes, I know who loves me.
Yes, I am quite blest.
Yes, I am at peace and more than you have ever guessed.

Yes, you should depart now.
Yes, you should just go.
Yes, my life is fine now and just how much you'll never know.

Cherie Burbach

Waiting Expectantly

I asked Today to leave
    I was busy with regret
    and so,
    had no time to entertain.

When Tomorrow came
    I asked it to wait quietly
    in the extra room
    with my good intentions
    and the apologies I would say
    when the time was right.

Yesterday tried to run away from me
    but I chased it until I caught up with it.
    I asked it to show itself over and over
    as I waited expectantly
    for a different result.

    Somehow, the more I watched
    the more beautiful it's
    cast of characters became.
    Those that left me
    seemed so much more handsome,
    while I seemed foolish and small.

Just then a hand held open
    the door to If Only,
    and I entered
    thinking that now
    all my saved up wishes
    would come true.

Cherie Burbach

The Story of Me

One day, not so long ago
>	when the challenges of this world
>	weighed heavy on me
>	and every day of life
>	seemed to be a struggle, a fight,

I screamed aloud
>	to the only one
>	who could possibly understand
>	and in my cries shouted,
>	"I can't fight this fight any longer!"

I expected Him to be angry
>	but to my surprise
>	He picked me up, dried my tears
>	and told me, the story, of me.

I sat curled in His arms
>	and as he read from this book, I saw,
>	on the cover, my picture,
>	for the title, my name
>	and the author, I noticed, was Him.

I read along with Him
>	and found myself interrupting as He spoke.
>	After all, I knew this story,
>	I'd lived it,
>	and didn't want to hear it again.

Once more, He was patient,
>	and continued with the story.
>	I saw each disappointment,
>	each blessing,
>	and the pain I'd embraced.

I squirmed in His arms,
>	feeling more like a failure,
>	but He held tight, saying,
>	"Wait, child, there's more."
>	So I listened again.

He turned the pages
>	and showed me
>	the lessons I'd learned
>	mapped out for me personally
>	in the way only I could understand.

He read the story
>	with pride,
>	and His love
>	made me cry
>	at my selfishness.

I paid close attention
>	to each word, each event,
>	as He read me
>	the story
>	of me.

Cherie Burbach

Anticipation
>overtook me
>and I held my breath
>as He neared the end
>of my personal tale.

And suddenly
>he stopped
>closed the book
>and with a smile, asked
>"Now what will you write?"

Silently I Read Mary Oliver's Poetry

Late at night
>as I read
>"More Beautiful Than the Honey Locust Tree
>Are the Words of the Lord"

I am filled with thoughts of Heaven
>as Mary Oliver
>with her beautiful words
>often evokes.

I am bursting with
>excitement
>and want of shouting,
>"Glory be to God!"

But I must remain quiet
>for my husband sleeps
>beside me.

I want to read aloud to him,
>"For You are forever
>while I am like a
>single day that passes."

But he sleeps so sound
>and looks so handsome
>and content
>in his dreams.

Cherie Burbach

He is my nature,
    my blessing,
    my gift of love.

And I smile at his gentle snores —
    my little slice of heaven.

Never Lost

1.
And there I am
embraced by people who love me,

most of them anyway,
except those with darkness inside them
who remind me that I'm different
who sneer with uncontainable joy
as they lie in wait,
aiming arrows filled with poison
at my young, impressionable, heart.

2.
And there I go
searching for people who left me,

some of them, anyway,
including those who were
too busy to love me
who sent me off on a boat
filled with holes,
smiling at the dock, waving good bye
before they turned and went back
to the ones they chose to keep.

Cherie Burbach

3.
And here I am
begging for people to accept me

one of them, anyway,
as the whispers about
my lack of education and upbringing
swirl through the air like locusts.
The gossip hits my back again and again
as I stand smiling in a white dress.

4.
And here you are,
pouring your grace on me,

some of it, anyway,
while the people who failed to welcome me
receive some
and the ones who couldn't love me
receive some
and
the ones who don't know
how much they need it
get the rest.

5.
And here I am,
finally with you

forever and always, anyway,
where I learn about
this path you sent me on.
Where I was part of one family,
then another, and when I tried
to find my way back again
you remind me
I was never lost.

Cherie Burbach

Home

H - hope filled
O - offering encouragement
M - making you feel special
E - ever faithful

Awake

It's like living in a dream
where words are fuzzy
actions happen and we attribute them
to someone else.

Like the dream where
the man you didn't know told you he was your father,
or where the lady you thought must be your friend
turned out to be a stranger…

So is the life
where you place your trust in people
who aren't who they say they are.

In the dream where you float above the clouds
thinking you're okay
and suddenly,
feel yourself falling…
faster and faster
until you wake up
thankful,
it was only a dream…

So goes the moment
you see
the one you thought you were safe from,
and you speak up,
get distance,
and wake up to your wiser life,
a bit shook, a bit scared,
but thankful all the same,
that now you're finally awake.

Cherie Burbach

Up

Uncertainty
nips at your heels.

Worries of
children money family jobs and friends
jab you,
push you in different directions.

You fall,
down to the ground
bury your head
and utter the smallest of prayers.
So low and uncertain you're not even sure
what you're asking.

But just when
you're about to let the hopelessness
nudge you all the way down,
a hand pulls you up.

Up
above the pain
above the tangled maze of doubt
that had you lost.

Up
to stand on your own two feet
to look in a new direction
to remind you
that you're not alone.

Up
so you can try again.

Cherie Burbach

By Poetry

I will write poetry today.

I will pull up my sadness by the string that winds its way around my soul.
I will pull until my heart is free from its weight,
and the string will tie words together which bring beauty in its place
and that heaviness that followed me everywhere
will be replaced by poetry.

The Wise Bride

I tied my shame to a post
then ran as far and as fast
as I could
until I was breathless,

hands on knees
drinking in
deep pockets of air
like the sweetest tea.

Each failure
and embarrassment
knotted tightly together
with my best ribbon.

Each step had pulled
that ribbon tight
until there were miles
between me and that post.

My shame hung up like
clothes on a laundry line
waving easily in the wind.
Each piece colorful, unique.

As I looked back
at the display
my past mistakes created
I saw truth, beauty, and growth.

Cherie Burbach

I felt them tug at my body
this ribbon still anchored
to my past at one end
and my present life at the other.

I could cut them loose and run,
leave them flying wildly to get lost,
landing on others who don't
know what to do with them.

Or I could go back
let them wind their way around me
over and over,
so tight that I can't breathe.

Instead, I tug, hard,
and the ribbon comes free from the poll
my mistakes and shame
fly openly behind me

like the train of a
beautiful wedding dress
worn by me,
the wise bride.

Hope

Hope
shines down from Heaven
even through the darkest night.

Hope is
is the secret ingredient
of dreams,

and the one confidant
you can safely share
your secrets with.

Hope whispers
try again, one more time
and see what happens.

It stands before you,
hands on hips,
and asks, "Why not you?"

Hope puts up a billboard
with your picture on it
that says, "Cherished one."

It acts like a pit crew
cleaning your view
when things look cloudy.

Hope shows you a new equation
when everyone says
the odds are against you.

Cherie Burbach

It turns your head
toward the future,
leaving the past behind.

Hope
smoothes out your confidence
so you don't trip,

like a maid of honor
holding the train
of your wedding gown,

and tosses breadcrumbs behind you
when you roam
so you can find your way back.

Hope
reminds us
that everyone's story
is different

and so it will never come
to your pity party
no matter how many times you ask.

Hope remembers
all your dreams
even when you've forgot them.

It runs to you,
breathless,
and says,

"I've been looking for you
everywhere"
when you're trying to hide.

Hope
views failure
as practice,

and says
not now,
but soon.

Cherie Burbach

Forgive

I embrace this life,
        as a child of God.

You may knock me down,
        but His love lifts me up.
You may bring pain into my life,
        but He comforts me.
You may laugh at my mistakes,
        but I embrace them, my personalized lesson.
You may hurt me,
        but I'll forgive you.

I'll forgive you
        because I'm loved by Him.

I'll forgive you
        because He will.

I'll forgive you
        so I can forgive myself.

I'll forgive you
        so I can be free.

All Right

Can it be
that the voice
you hear
when you
turn away
from
the noise
and listen
to your life
is not

guilt
or
your mother
or the
shoulda
woulda
coulda's

but the voice
of God
urging you
to be still
reassuring you
that when
you feel alone,
think you might
be crazy,
you're alright.

Cherie Burbach

That it is
all going to be
all right.

New Path

Today,

I threw my calendar away.
Tossed it on the pile
with my expectations and
the judgement of others.

I lit a match,
and smiled as the flames
ripped through the paper
like a toddler having his
very best temper tantrum.

My face warmed
at the heat
which grew stronger
as the papers shriveled
and died,
returning to ashes.

As the last ember flickered
I felt the weight of my plans,
the heaviness of a life
scheduled out,
become lighter, softer,
until it too disappeared.

Cherie Burbach

All that was left
was me,
standing in an office
with a big desk and
phone and computer,
and just beyond them,
a window.

The sun shined on a path
that led from
my office door.
A path I had never been on.
Until now.

Blaming the Sun

She fell short of her goals
reaching the halfway point,
and forgot to be thankful
for the half she had reached.

She tried again and got taken
in a different direction,
blaming the road that remained unmoved
instead of the feet that took her there.

Do you blame the sun
for disappearing each night,
when it is us that
turns our back on it?

Cherie Burbach

Roberta

I see you there
filled with confidence
thinking you can
take on the world.

You're not afraid
of the things I am.
You're right in the middle
of a large family

that keeps you busy
and gives you distance
from the loneliness
that chased you all your life.

You love your big brothers,
your cherished sister,
and you love
yourself, too.

I envy you a bit.
Envy that
I never got
to be you,

never got to be
that kind of strong
or know the self-confidence
you would have.

But I know
that our lives
the ones we
actually lived

are all that matters.
The what ifs
and if only's
are fool's gold.

You would
have had
issues,
too.

Different issues
than me.
Everyone has them
and so would have you.

Dear Roberta,
I carry you
with me

because it allows me
to offer fondness
to strangers
and call them family.

Cherie Burbach

Your real existence faded
each year I grew up
into the world
I'd been placed,

but I hold
you dearly
in my
heart.

I'm Not That Girl

I'm not that girl
      the one you knew?

Who smiled when I hurt
      and slapped away your kind hands.

I'm not that girl
      who'd rather self-destruct
      than ask for help.

I'm not her.
      Not anymore.

I'm not that girl
      who chased sorrow
      and ran away from everything good.

I'm not that girl
      you thought you knew.
            But no one did.
                  Not even me.

Cherie Burbach

Father's Eyes

In my father's eyes
    I am lazy
    and slow.
    I have a long way to go, and then,
    I still won't be close.

In my father's eyes
    I am loud
    and sarcastic.
    My voice makes a shrill cacophony of chaos,
    at last, I had nothing important to say.

In my father's eyes
    I see why
    they treat me so.
    I deserve it,
    I really do.

In my father's eyes
    I am not the answer
    for his deep despair.
    And so I think,
    why am I here?

In The Father's eyes
    I have come so far.
    And beauty and happiness
    will be my reward
    from now until forever.

In The Father's eyes
      You can't hurt me.
      His grace protects me;
      His love sustains me.

In The Father's eyes
      I'm His child.
      His delight.
      He wants me here,
      and I belong.

Cherie Burbach

Our Beautiful Brokenness

What if at the end Jesus says
"Yes, you were right,
they were wrong,
and here is why it does not matter"

What if you could
embrace the warmth of the sun,
feel the pull of the moon,
and see the living waters
of our world,
all from your perch
up on the brightest star

What if Jesus
brushed your doubts away
like tiny specs of dust
on an old record,
and gave you a new song
to sing instead

What if He could
show you His scars
and in them you see
His heartbreak
caused by each one of
your thoughts
of self-doubt

What if I get to Heaven
and Jesus tells me
that the joke I'd told once,
the one meant to make
people laugh
but only ended up
offending them
really *was* funny.
He got it.

What if He tells me
I'm beautiful,
and does it in such a way
that I'll never
have to look in a mirror again.

What if Jesus tells me
that all those times I cried
and screamed His name,
He was there, holding me.
That if He hadn't been there,
I would have run off,
done something crazy.
But instead, I cried for a while,
dried my tears,
and went back out into
the world that had hurt me.

Cherie Burbach

What if I look back
on my life and see
my brokenness,
my path paved with mistakes,
and Jesus nods proudly
and says,
"Yes! Isn't it beautiful?"

What if the why's
of your life
were answered in an instant,
your understanding
the final gift
that allowed you
to finally feel His grace.

Poiema: New and Selected Poems

Chapter 2:

Embracing His Divine Purpose

Yes, You

Hey you
pretty girl,
yes *you*...
... the one who doesn't feel so pretty,
and is long past being called a girl.

While you were checking out
the lines on your face,
God was telling you how beautiful
you are to Him.
He sent a cool breeze to caress your face.
Did you feel it?

Hey you
silly girl,
yes *you*...
... the one who has been fretting
over those ten pounds you gained.

God is telling you to go outside
and enjoy the sunshine He provided.
He sent a bluebird to chirp outside your window.
Did you hear it?

Hey you
talented girl,
yes *you*...
... the one who gave up your dream
all those years ago.

Cherie Burbach

God is reminding you that
He gave you all those creative gifts
before you were even born.
He sent you a nudge in the form of inspiration.
Did you sense it?

Hey you
graceful girl,
yes *you*...
... the one who wastes her time on
everything she doesn't have.

God sent His son for you,
to remind you of all the good that awaits you.
Or did you forget?

Our New Home

They placed
us here,
you and me

in with the other swimmers
in this vast
and lovely sea.

We floundered for a while
as one strong current
carried us in opposite directions.

We even sunk below the surface at times,
and struggled to catch our breath
while water filled our ears and mouth

as other swimmers
grabbed our arms and legs
and pulled us down.

We gulped for air
and tried to save those
who tugged at us.

We used all our might
to pull them up,
those strangers who shared our lives.

But even though we tried to teach them how
to kick and paddle their way around the water
they refused to budge.

Cherie Burbach

They held our feet
while we struggled to keep
ourselves afloat.

Finally we had to kick free, push them away
until we could use the strength we had left,
and float back to the surface.

We drifted awhile,
resting our tired bodies
until our strength could come back.

And when we'd caught our breath
and could swim again on our own,
we finally saw the way that would take us to dry land.

This time, we went with the current,
and found that it propelled us forward
at a dizzying speed.

We knew then
we'd make it
to the safety of shore.

But first,
we sought
them out.

We could still hear their cries in our ears,
not pleas for help,
but demands for assistance.

And though we tried to help them,
we could only point to the shore
and suggest they swim along with us.

And we prayed for their safety,
you and I,
while we left the cold, dark sea, and headed home.

Cherie Burbach

What I Didn't Know

What I didn't know
as those self-destructive habits
ruled the way in which I lived
holding court
like an ancient queen
regal, mighty,
yet out of touch with her subjects…

What I didn't know
during the times
I'd run toward
the shortest path to the end,
was that I'd never
be successful in my goal to stay down…

What I didn't know
was that I had a silent barrier
surrounding me day and night.
It followed me everywhere,
and though I could not see it,
refused to let me fall…

What I didn't know
was that you were faithful
and in your prayers
included me;
asking above all else that
I be protected
from evil,
and wrong,
and sometimes, myself…

What I didn't know
back then
is everything I am thankful for
today.

Cherie Burbach

Take My Hand

When I was small
and the world was so scary and big,
you took my hand
to help me cross the street.

As a teenage girl
I cried over taunts
about my full round face,
and you took my hand
and told me to smile anyway,
that you thought I was beautiful.

When I struggled with work
and long hours, low pay, and poor bosses,
you took my hand,
and listened.

And though I never told you
how my father's hand had stung my face,
how my despair multiplied with his addiction,
you took my hand,
and saw the little girl who got left behind.

When so many years passed
and we realized you were leaving us,
I thanked you for how special you are,
and took your hand,
to tell you it was okay to go.

And as you left,
and I held your hand,
and took comfort in the fact
that one day,
you'd be there
to take my hand, again.

Cherie Burbach

Angel In Waiting

Sometimes she'd remember me
        and be waiting at the door
        arms folded
        and frowning.
She'd tell me I was late
        ask me where I'd been.
        I'd say it was 6:00
        that I always came at 6:00
        she'd shrug
        then smile at the food I brought
        already forgetting why she was angry.

I'd set the table
        the good china from great grandma
        the good silverware.
She'd ask if it was a holiday
        her memory sparked
        noticing the distinction
        between special and every day.
And I'd tell her no
        just a special day to be with her
        she'd nod
        hesitantly
        then eat the food I'd prepared.
Sometimes she'd turn up her nose
        but eat heartily just the same.
Sometimes she'd say things like
        she didn't realize chicken
        went with spaghetti
        and I would smile
        because chicken and spaghetti
        were still words she recognized.

We would not talk about
    things inevitable
    as if we could anyway.
We'd talk
    about things we could
    like the wind to a sailboat
    our conversation would change direction
    depending on where
    her memory took us.
Some days
    she would talk of things she knew
    her eyes like bright shining stars.
Some days
    she was unsure
    of her life, her memories, of here and now
    her eyes blank and fearful
    looking for my assurance
    so she could go on.

But each night
    as my friends
    lived their youth
    dancing, dreaming, falling in love,
    I would sit by her side
    watching her eat
    taking pride
    in the pretty table
    the cloth napkins
    the salt shaker that was for special occasions.

Cherie Burbach

Each night
    I would make this dinner
    and made everything about it special.
I would
    forget about work
    and realize this was real
    and the most important thing
    I could do
for this woman
    who once took my hand
    and taught me to crochet
    and now reached for my hand
    to steady herself.
It was what I could do
    for this angel in waiting.

Seasons of Life and Big Girl Tears

Hello HALF CENTURY MARK!
I am using all caps for you,
because you're
a big thing.

You're something that is looming
a mere weeks away
and you are feeling enormous
and pretty awful.
If I'm being honest,
I've shed a few tears.
Okay, more than a few.
It's not because I'm aging
or that my body
is doing different (weird) things
or even that someone might look at me
and say, "You're 50! Eeek!"
No, it's that 50 is
pushing up memories,
like a stubborn diver
determined to have you look
at buried artifacts
found on a ship
that went down
years and years ago.

Those things
that were precious to me
then are now covered in rust,
and not so shiny and perfect
anymore.

Cherie Burbach

Yet this big 50
is down there,
diving mask on
and kicking furiously
to bring up things
that are better left buried.
Like self-doubt.
And feeling worthless.
And wondering why
some things in my life
that should have been easy
were hard.
I haven't felt this way
in a while.
Darn 50.

I'm feeling
the seasons of life,
going to sleep at night
dreaming of images
that have become my art.

I wake up
with thoughts of
strong women with deep roots
who sway in the wind
and might lose their leaves
a time or two
but never, ever
completely break.
And each time
unpleasant thoughts
crowd my heart,
tears come
to wash them away.

They don't celebrate
the negativity.
They do their business
like my grandma
would dust the furniture,
with a quick and mighty hand,
a nod to a job well done,
and an attitude that says, "Moving on."

These are big girl tears.
Ones that wash me
clean of regret,
wipe away longing,
and instead give me
the gift of a life
without expectation.

These big girl tears
force my hands away
from gripping things
that still trip me up.

Rather than holding on
to past whatevers
I am wiping away these tears
and readjusting my focus.
When the water clears,
a new vision emerges,
one that says
welcome to the woman
you were meant to be all along.

Cherie Burbach

Rise Above That Past So Dark

There is, perhaps, a quiet
small voice that you have heard,
that whispers "come on… try it…
…'cause I won't say a word."

The voice leans in so closely,
you feel it in your soul.
It tells you lies, well mostly,
so you'll follow down the hole.

Farther, farther… on you go,
'till you forget about your home.
Falling faster… down so low,
to the bottom, where you'll roam.

Hard to find your way back now,
hard to recognize the truth.
How did this happen? When? How?
The voice stole away your youth.

Take comfort in this truth, my friend,
though the voice had called to you.
It's not over, 'til the end,
you can always start anew.

Rise above that past, so dark,
turn away from that demon's voice.
Move on now, and make your mark.
With your future, you have a choice.

The Basket

She heard someone at the door
and as she answered it
saw a basket on the doorstep.
A baby? She wondered.

She picked up the basket,
light as air,
and as she carried it inside,
noticed it was empty
except for a note, which read,
"Your problems. Here."

She shook her head.
Read it again.
Folded the paper,
and put it back in the basket.

Problems?
She laughed,
then grabbed
the note again.

It was balled up,
the paper crinkled
from where she had
smashed it in her hand.

She smoothed it out,
read it again.
This time it said:
"Toss them in."

She dropped the paper,
tried to clear her thoughts.
What was this? A joke?
She shook her head again.

But she pictured her problems,
and picking up the paper again,
silently thought of each one.
Then she crumbled the paper
and tossed it into the basket.
She turned to go,
wanted to leave the paper
and the basket behind,
but struggled to walk away.

She reached for the paper again.
This time it read,
"Yes. Right here.
Don't worry.
I can hold them."

She got a little cocky.
Sure, sure, she thought,
I'll give you my problems!
Here!
She tossed the paper in the basket.

"Ready?" She asked sarcastically.
"Okay then, how about this?
My mortgage is overdue.
My husband took off,
and I can't make
ends meet by myself.
And I'm angry!
Is that a problem?
Because if it is,
you can take that, too."

She waited.
Folded her arms and frowned.
Finally she turned,
slammed the door
and went inside.

That night,
she slept,
fitfully, deeply.
The first time that had
happened in months.

As she woke,
she thought of the basket,
and ran to see
if it was still there.

Cherie Burbach

She opened the door,
and the basket now held
a bouquet of flowers.
She reached down
and smelled their
beautiful fragrance,
smiled to herself,
and brought the basket
inside.

Worry

Did you think worrying was an activity –
        it takes up space
        it fills your life
        it pushes today away.

You swallow it whole –
        empty calories
        chewing on what might be
        what could be
        what may be
        filling you up.

Too full –
        to drink life's wine.

Too full –
        to sit beneath the stars and listen.

Too full –
        consumed
        with what might happen
        if you left your house, your world
        and tasted
                what others must swallow each day.

Cherie Burbach

What may be –
      what might be
      fills your ears
      fills you up so full
      you get sick
      your stomach aches
      no room
            for nourishment.

So full –
      that you wither
      from malnourishment
      become sick
      and cease to live.

So full –
      and yet
            hungry still.

Fallen Short

At first
>when I needed help
>you turned your head.

Why bother
>you thought,
>what's in it for you?

As time went on
>and my struggles grew
>you smiled when you saw me
>then laughed behind my back.

What's wrong with me,
>you asked anyone aloud.

And when
>I fell so low
>so very low
>you let me sit before you
>broken,
>my fears, my failures, my saddened past
>laid out for you
>helplessly
>shamefully.

Everyone's watching,
>you realized at last.

Cherie Burbach

You gave me your hand
    and thought how good
    you looked
    while I rose up an inch
    not quite to my feet.

And while I struggled to stand erect,
    you dropped my hand.
        But no one was looking then.

And now
    that I stand firmly
    on my own two feet
    you tell the world
    it was you
    who led me all the way up
    making them believe
    that you really cared.

Not even seeing
    that you were the one
    who walked away.

But I know
    it was me,
    with strength from the one above
    the muscles in my legs
    pushing me up
        from the cold, dark ground.

He helped me do that,
    not you.

How Will I Find You Again?

How will I find you again,
after I waited so long to hold you?
How will I know where to look,
when I'm not sure where you have gone?

How will I see you again,
when we go to our new destination?
How will I know your face,
when it's your soul that will hold your smile?

How will I know you're alright,
if you start your journey before me?
How will I find you again,
if you don't call out my name as you leave?

How will I find you, all over again,
and the peace from your love and strength?
How will I find my way?
If you go, then take me with you.

Cherie Burbach

You Should Know

You should know
that I love you
even now
after what you said and did
despite our short time together.

You should know
that I've forgiven us
you and me both
but I'm sad
over what we became.

You should know
that I've moved on
because I had to
but if you wanted to try again
I would.

Is That All There Is

In a cafe sat two women,
each about thirty-five.
They each drank cups of coffee
as they thought about their life.

Is that all there is, thought the one aloud,
is that all that life can be?
My husband, my kids, and a dinner meal,
is that all there is for me?

Her thoughts went on, now silently,
as she thought about her past.
I once dreamed of a big career,
but the years have passed so fast.

I'm too old to find my path
my direction's been preordained.
If I'd only started sooner
oh the goals I'd have attained.

Oh why did I not start it then
with plentiful years ahead?
I could have spoke at conferences
when now 'I do' is all I've said.

Is that all there is, I beg to know,
is that all that life can be?
I could have had so much more
than housework and kids to feed.

Cherie Burbach

While she drank her joe, the other girl
looked down at her lap and sighed.
Is this my whole life, she wondered,
is that all there is, she cried.

If she could go back now and change her path
she knew at last, she would.
I'd say yes and I do to the question he asked,
I'd be married all these years if I could.

I thought I was too young back then
to be thought of as a wife.
But I'd trade this job and paycheck
and have a husband and kids in my life.

How wrong my independence was,
how I'd change it if given the chance.
If I knew then what I now know,
I'd trade without a backward glance.

Is that all there is, I wonder now,
is this all my life can be?
Success with utter loneliness,
is that all there is for me?

They both looked at their watches
and no longer could they stay.
Is that all there is... each one thought
as they headed on their way.

Do You Love Me?

Do you love me?
I asked.
And you said,
"Yes, I think I do."

You brought me flowers that day,
for no good reason whatsoever.
Just because.

Do you love me?
I asked again,
and smiled at the ring on my finger.
And you said,
"Yes, I really do."

You looked at reception halls and flower books that day,
even though I knew you didn't care
about those things like I did.

Do you really, really, love me,
I wondered.
And before I could ask, you said,
"I take this woman to have and to hold
in sickness and in health."

You cried tears of joy that day,
as we were introduced as man and wife.

Cherie Burbach

How can you love me!
I shouted.
And you yelled,
"There's nothing you can do to make me stop!"

You took me in your arms that day,
and told me it would be all right.

Will you still love me?
I wept.
And you said,
"Now more than ever."

You made love to me that day,
even though my body had changed,
and wrinkles made their way across my face.

I love you, more than anything in this world,
you said.
And I smiled as I thought,
"I know."

I thanked God for the most precious gift
of my life that day.
I thanked Him for you.

Happily Ever After

Happily ever after is

waking up next to the one you love
holding hands as you watch TV
cooking dinner just so someone can say, "You made my favorite meal."
lying awake as your loved one snores next to you
sharing housework
worrying over money
praying for each other
making love
laughing at private jokes
arguing about how much butter is on the popcorn
holding someone after a nightmare
talking about the best movie plots of all time
playing cards on a rainy Sunday
doing crafts
listening to someone vent after a long day
being so very proud of someone
wondering how you lived before you met someone
going back to the coffee shop where you met, just so you can relive the day your life changed forever

Happily ever after is
every single moment with you.

Cherie Burbach

Filled With Your Spirit

A man up front bows his head,
respectfully, dutifully,
while the woman next to him
sings softly,
a smile alight on her face.

The girl next to me raises her arms,
her palms, stretched up… up,
as if she is trying to
reach you in Heaven.

And me? I sing loudly, off-key,
while tears stream down my face.
My heart is filled with joy
because you love me.

I am filled with your spirit,
and so are they,
and we are blest.

Each Time You Smile

There is a ray
of sunlight
that shines brighter
each time
you smile.

Cherie Burbach

Marriage

A gift
      wrapped up in a morning kiss
      an embrace, then exchange of wishes
      for good things to happen today.

A call
      in a workday afternoon
      details told of each other's everyday
      I love you's sent out on a phone line.

A journey
      in the long ride made each night
      problems falling further behind
      with each mile closer to a shared address.

A smile
      to see lights on and dinner cooking
      a sense of peace and wonder
      to know there is someone waiting for you
      there.

A life
      wrapped up in small details
      and a love that says
      welcome home.

Dear Women

Dear women of this world,
      I support you
      I champion you
      I love you.

This is the thought we must carry
in our minds and hearts.

Cherie Burbach

The Cost of Addiction

You sir
with the three-piece suit
and the whiskey on your breath.

You there
with the smile so cute
and the skin that looks like death.

Young man
with the yellow teeth
and the anger in your face.

And you
living on the edge
at your breakneck, crazy pace.

You all
share a common trait
as you grapple with your vice.

Respect
though it feels like hate,
as your life now pays the price.

Family Nap

Mid-afternoon
a rainy Sunday
the kind of day where
you don't feel guilty
taking a nice long nap.

My favorite blanket,
the one
my granny made for me
when I was ten
wraps me with warmth.

My husband cuddles
next to me,
his hand finds its way
under my shirt.

He pulls me close
as our sleepy selves
drift off to dreamland.
Our little doggie Genevieve
snuggles up
find a place she likes
at the foot of the bed
then lays her tiny head
on my foot
and sleeps.

Cherie Burbach

As we each find comfort
in the serenity of our family,
we dream peacefully.
Each heading
off to our own
version of fantasy
while we remain safe
in each other's arms.

The Suicides

They break our hearts
with their inability to see
the beauty in life,
the small moments
that catch your breath
remind you what God created,
and make you stop long enough
to pull yourself from
the dark abyss of hopelessness
and press on.

They confuse us
when they laugh,
tell us they're okay
and keep their pain
hidden away.
Like a dress you
put up in the attic,
waiting to pull it out
on a random day
when you find yourself
sick of how you look and act
and just need something old and familiar
to cover yourself,
no matter how much it doesn't fit.

Cherie Burbach

They scare us
with their sadness, determination.
We fear the path they took
and want a map of their steps
so we can choose a different way.

They anger us
when they give up.
We want them here
because we are here.
We are here and why isn't that enough
to keep them here?
Don't they want to stay for us? With us?

They sadden us
when we realize their dark choice
made in an instant
will stay with us,
haunt us,
with a guilt so intense
that will wonder
what we could have said,
what could we have done…
forever.

They motivate us
with the permanence of their end.
We see the fragility of life,
watch the ones we love
vanish so quickly
we might have even forgotten
they were here,
were it not for the hole in our hearts
that they left behind.

They break our hearts
over and over again,
when we realize
they are gone,
and there's nothing more
we can do.

Cherie Burbach

I Send Out My Prayers

I send out my prayers
to those women
so young
who timidly ask for approval.

I see their uncertainty
when criticized for being
beautiful
ugly
fat
slow to speak
loud
and unlike the perception
of those who assume.

I send out my hopes
to those women
so foolish
who haven't yet realized
the trail of mistakes behind them.

I see their confidence
when they think they're
accepted
loved
cherished
respected
because they did
what someone told them to do.

I send out my experience
to those women
so unsure
who wonder if
they'll find the true path to love.

I see their genuine beauty shine,
even when others
scream at them
hit them
ignore them
deceive them
simply because they can.

I send out my love
to all women
so young, so old, so kind, so bold,
who need to forgive
so they can move on.

I see their apprehension and pain
when others
preach to them
gossip about them
look down their nose at them
because they believe they are superior,
and are too ignorant to see that they
should bring these women
all women
up.
Not tear them down.

Cherie Burbach

The Mentor

Her hair has grayed,
her face is lined,
and her mirror has changed
from a looking glass
to the smiles she sees
in the ones she loves.

Her wealth is measured on
the friends who hold her dear,
and the silent gratitude
of those she listened to,
and prayed for.

Her own heartaches
washed away
by the love of a generation
that she
may never meet.

Her advice,
sprinkled into the lives of young women,
encouraging their strengths,
slowly and gently sowing the seeds
for a mature and balanced future.

Princess

P - peace loving
R - real
I - intelligent
N - noble
C - creative
E - extraordinarily bright
S - sensitive
S - special

Cherie Burbach

Simple Kindness

I see God
in the smile that comes
suddenly and unexpectedly
from a stranger,

just when I think
I'm not worthy,
my failures and ineptitude
so far reaching

that they
cloak my face
yet leave
my body naked.

Just then
when I think
God has forgotten
about me

as I walk
through a crowd
surrounded by others
who are all too deserving

of love and gratitude
and thus,
more important
to God,

the face of a stranger
rushes by
yet stops,
for a moment,

as our eyes meet
and my existence
is validated
as if to say

I see you
and
you're important
to Him.

Cherie Burbach

This House Had

This house had
a puppy,
who filled this space
with joy, even as she
chewed our books
and furniture,

then grew to be
the family dog
who brought us smiles
and demonstrated
unconditional love.

This house had
a newly married couple
who loved and fought
and learned to cling
to God and each other,

who lived joyfully
and celebrated
a decade together
with genuine surprise
that time had flown so fast.

This house had
homemade meals,
holiday memories,
family reunions,

and many, many
visits from friends,
all of whom
laughed and cried,
prayed and rejoiced.

This house had
all the people and pets
and faith and love
to make it
a home,
but it didn't have you.

Cherie Burbach

Loved by the Creator

She is
loved by the creator
of those dimples nestled in her smile,
of her grateful heart,
and joyful soul.

Loved by the creator
of her wicked sense of humor
and the ability to laugh
loudly and unashamed.

Loved, she is, so loved
by this creator
who taught birds how to sing
and placed the sun in the
perfect spot in the sky.

Loved by the creator
who gives us the moon
to keep us company
at night,
who holds us,
even when we think
we're all alone.

She is loved by the same creator
as the mountains she admires
in the distance,
the stars she gazes at
each night,
her favorite flower
that she places in a vase
beside her bed,
and the horizon,
placed just beyond her reach.

Loved by the creator
of her many friendships,
hopeful spirit,
and ability to make
a joyful noise.

Loved by the creator
who makes no mistakes,
who said,
"My world needs you,"
and who hears her prayers
and holds them dear.

Cherie Burbach

Granny

We said our goodbyes
in a funeral home
with stuffy curtains
and much too somber music.

We were sad, of course,
because you were gone
but we rejoiced
at your long life.

We gathered together,
all of us, a rare event,
spread out
as we are

but we came together
to mourn
but also celebrate
this family you made.

And as the cousins
all left
returning home
I fell asleep

and dreamt
that you were standing
at the end
of my bed.

You smiled
that sweet smile
and then looked surprised
making an "O" with your lips

because you didn't
think I'd be able
to see you
from where you were then.

And *where* we you?
Heaven?
On your way?
I've always wondered.

I shouted,
in my dreams
I love you, Granny!
I love you!

and as I did, woke myself up,
still staying
I love you
over and over and over.

What a nice way
to say our final goodbye,
on this side,
at least.

Cherie Burbach

Truth

Truth
is the only bird
whose song
gets louder
or softer
depending
on the listener.

Breath of Life

I want to sit at the
foot of my Father

wiped clean from sin
where the gentle love of
my creator washes
me from this world
and births me into the
one that lasts forever

where I will finally see
the good that was
intended for me
and be embraced
as the child
He wanted

so much that He
breathed her into existence.

Cherie Burbach

Women's March

She didn't understand
the older woman
outside her window,
marching on the pavement below,
angry sign hoisted high
into the air.

The woman looked silly to her.
She was too busy for that.
She had a life.

She shouted out her window,
"You look ridiculous!
I don't feel marginalized!
I am in charge of my own life!
My own choices!
Why don't you go read a book!
Help orphans!
Care for the needy!
Your marching is…"

She stopped,
shook her head,
slammed the window.

But she couldn't look away.
The woman remained,
putting down her sign,
and waving up at the girl.

She opened the window again.
"What!"

The woman called up to her,
"I'm glad you don't get it.
That's why I marched.
That's why I still do.
So you don't ever
have to understand
what it is I've felt
and experienced
at the hands of men."

The girl stood still,
holding back an eye roll
for fear the woman would see it.

The woman waved again.
"Thank you, honey!
You've showed me
everything I've done mattered.
Thank you.
Now, go back to your life!"
She picked up her sign again.
"I've got this!"

Cherie Burbach

Children of the World

Children,

I spend time with you
because I want to teach you
all I've learned.
And then,
learn from you all the things
I had forgotten.

I've loved you, always,
and yet, I was scared.
The thought of doing to you
what was done to me
frightened me beyond measure.

I wondered if I'd be a good mother.
But nature took away my choice
on bringing you into the world,
and decades of grief
will follow me as long
as I have breath.

And yet,
there are times when I see
that even this is
a blessing for me.

My infertility a God-given
wall of protection
meant to keep my soul whole
against the stabs of memory
that would tear my heart in two.

You see, I can't look at you now
without the painful knowledge
that I was once
a child, too.

Your existence provides proof
that I was once small.

When memories show me
the slaps that would
knock me down

or the times hot, angry breath
told me how worthless I was,

there is a part of me
that thinks I couldn't possibly
have been that sweet and tiny,

and when I see you,
I know that I, too,
was once in need of careful handling
and that thought shatters
my heart to pieces.

So perhaps it is better
that I don't have
one of you
precious creatures
myself.

Perhaps that is what
has kept
my soul from floating away
from me
altogether.

Instead,
I close my mind
to the memory and smile
at you instead,
and this keeps me
moving forward.

Children of the world,
I know you see me
just as I am.

You see the good
and the nerdy,
the odd and the cool,
and you accept me
for it all.

I am one more person
in your life
to talk to,
to sing songs with,
and to care about you.

As I cheer you on
you might even see me
as the little girl
I once was.

Only you would be able
to look beyond
the fear in my eyes
to hear the giggle that was
meant to come out
a lifetime ago.

It plays for you
somewhere in the space
only you can hear.

Children of the world,
I love you.
More than that,
I value you.

You are important,
you are needed,
and you are
worthy.

Cherie Burbach

Tree Girl

The summers of her life
were carefree and light,
yet there were times
when the sun's blaze
pounded down on her,
causing her to get lazy
and bored
with her blessings.
Even then
her earnest prayers
could not be withered
by the blaze of the sun.
Fall brought
memories of school
the feeling of starting over,
but she watched helplessly
as the leaves
were brushed away
by the winds of change.
Could she bend
without breaking?
Would she remember
the solidness of her roots?
She held tight,
sure that she would wither,
while she stood her ground,
reminding herself
she was worthy
and deserved to be loved.

Winter
left her shaking, cold,
trying to find the place
where she could
warm her spirits again.
It was the
coldest, darkest
season of her life.
In the distance
they could see
her light shine,
even though
she couldn't
see it herself.

So while the cold
came rushing back,
it could not match
her powerful light.
She wandered forward,
**physically and emotionally,
through life.**

Unsure
of where she was headed
or who would be there
waiting on the other side
when the cold air
slowly faded away
and light began to thaw
her hands and heart.

Cherie Burbach

The wandering
felt endless,
but as she looked back
she saw it was
only a season.

Soon,
she understood her talents,
embraced her purpose.
Winter years
gave way
to a warmer spring,
where she wandered
in the cold no more.

Our Beauty

Our beauty
lies not on our faces
smiling, toothpaste grins
of perfection,

showing the world
that we're good,
examples of
impeccable life choices.

It lies not
in the way
our children
say please and thank you,

or how our husbands
hold out their hands
and ask us
to dance at the church social.

Our true beauty
is not seen
when we
stand like statues.

holding our shame close
to our bodies
fearful of
dropping a piece.

Cherie Burbach

We're scattered,
we fail,
there are cracks
in our confidence

that let His light
shine through our souls,
which He designed
to last forever.

Some Children

Some children
must travel

before they
find their way
home.

Cherie Burbach

I Once Believed

I understand now
you're minimizing
my efforts

making digs
to imply
the good fortune

came from
somewhere
else.

It couldn't have
come from me,
because if it did

you'd have to
congratulate me
or at least

admit
you were wrong
and we can't have that.

It's okay.
I know who you are
now.

I once thought
you were someone
I needed
for approval.

Silence

There is sometimes a single
opportunity to remain silent,
focusing only on another, the one
who will tell you what you've
been misunderstanding,
what you've skipped over
and ignored.

This opportunity will come in wordlessly
and failure to recognize it will
leave you outside,
in the cold winds of
loneliness, as the faint cry
of self-awareness blows past you,
and too late, too late,
you'll feel it slip through
your fingers as you try and grab it.

Gone is the occasion to take things
from good to great
from casual to close
from average to worthy.
Gone, then, is
the marriage, the friendship, the relationship.

Cherie Burbach

Red-Tailed Hawk and Gray Wolf

1.

I watch my sister the red-tailed hawk,
soar above me.

I cry out to her, my throat aching,
but she is gone, eyes focused
on the rodent below her that she will
snatch off the ground and attack,
focused on her hunger, her need.

A piece of red feather and
the sound of her wings flapping
are all I have left.

I hold the feather tightly
unwilling to let go.
This is a part of her,
but it is a part of me too, isn't it?

2.

I take flight, eyes searching for her,
and instead, spot my brother,
the gray wolf.
He tells me I am not a bird, like my sister,
I am a wolf, and belong in his pack.

Can't I see the gray coat on my back?
Can't I feel the warm fur?

He nods, settling the matter, and moves forward,
an indication that I should follow,
but as they gather for dinner,
I stumble, unfamiliar with the
rituals of their group,
feeling even more alone
as I watch them together,
comfortable in their routines,
growling and hissing, and yet,
content with each other.

As they leave, searching for food,
I feel a hollow ache,
wondering if they searched for me
with the same enthusiasm.

Cherie Burbach

3.

I leave again, seeing for the first time
my gray fur, like theirs,
wondering why I never noticed before.
And yet I cling to the red feather
left behind by my sister,
flapping it as she would
and find myself flying again.

I see the grass that changes to snow and then mud.
I see the trees that turn from green to red to
completely bare.
I see birds shivering in the cold and wonder
if my sister is among them, but I know,
as surely as I know the sound of my own soul's cry,
that she is still hunting in a low tree
somewhere in the distance,
waiting patiently to steal the prey from another bird
to reap the reward of their dedication.

She is not struggling in the winter cold.

4.

I feel a pull as I fly,
as if I am a kite, being reeled in
closer and closer to the ground
by a creature I don't recognize.

I land among the colors,
each one looking different and odd,
as they show me my bed and give me
something to eat.

They tell me this is where I belong
and I look at the sea of incongruent faces
as they smile widely at each other
talking about their similar manner,
their eyes, their feet,
admiring all the things they think they are.

A chill comes over me,
wondering if I am in a dream,
seeing masks instead of faces,
hearing echoes instead of
the voices of home.

5.

Where, Lord, am I supposed to be?

I cry out,
tears running down my face.
I feel myself flying again
up, above the colors,
where I can see the creatures
from a higher view
and I close my eyes and hear you, Lord,
whispering for me to look.

You show me their entire lives,
you show me the gray wolves looking
up with concern,
and the red-tailed hawk, alone.

You offer me a cool bath,
made from the tears you kept,
each drop filled with your love.

You show me that I am
part of the gray wolf
and the creatures filled with colors
and the red-tailed hawk,
but I am also apart from them.
I belong and don't belong.
I am part of a family and alone.

6.

I still hold the red feather,
clinging to it as if it was my sister,
but realizing it is only a memory,
the moment I begged her to stay
and pulled her wings to get her
to take me with her,
but she had her own destiny to carry.

It was not fear of losing her
that caused me to grip that feather so tight,
but fear that I might lose myself
before I even knew who I was.

As God bathed me with love
I saw that the fur from the gray wolf
had kept me warm,
the creatures with masks helped me see
that I was a child of God,
and the red-tailed hawk
showed me that, I too, could fly.

7.

It was then that I finally
dropped the feather,
and as the brilliant red went softly
and slowly down, for the first time,
I looked up, unburdened.

Cherie Burbach

This Is the Moment

This moment is where you decide to be kind, rather than apathetic, hurried, or rushed.
It is where you make time rather than deciding you don't have time.
It is where you see that life is about to turn one way or the other, so you make the choice that will sit well with your soul.

This is the moment you decide to listen, rather than just waiting your turn to talk.
It is the moment you decide you got a second chance, and this time, you won't squander it, thinking you'll have another and another and another.

This is the moment you will follow the path of grace.
It is the moment you see you've been trying so hard to fit in, when you should have been welcomed in with open arms instead.

This is the moment you decide to stop giving your time and attention to those who will never give you theirs unless you whine and remind and beg.
This is the moment you stand, look up for guidance, and be the person God wants you to be rather than society and your friends and well-meaning people who just don't get it.

This is the moment, your entire life.

Could It Be

Friends to start
>we agree
>>we'll take it slow
>>but could it be?

Your hand on mine
>a smile for me
>>my brand new friend
>>but could it be?

You hold my glance
>eternity
>>I know we said…
>>but could it be?

You fell in love
>but not with me
>>you met someone
>>how could it be?

Cherie Burbach

Perfect Love

Perfect love
   comes not at first site
   with white horses and knights
   but quietly, gently,
   nudging it's participants along the way.

Perfect love
   comes from a nervous boy
   who debates a goodnight kiss
   and a cynical girl
   who never used to believe in ever after.

Perfect love
   brings with it harmony and poise
   transforming echoes of fears past
   to peace,
   and contentment.

Perfect love
   comes not from perfect people
   but from souls that find each other
   across a lifetime
   and unite to discover the future.

I Could Make Believe

I could cry in my pillow,
      pretend it's your shoulder.
I could pull my covers close,
      and think of your arms holding me tight.

I could make believe that I was loved by someone like you.

I could lay down my weary head
      and believe you're here
      to hold me as I dream.
I could pretend that you're
      just in the next room
      making sure all the lights are turned off
      before you come to bed.

I could make believe I was loved by you.

I could make believe
      this emptiness inside
      is just me missing you.
      That you'll be home. Soon.

I could make believe I was loved.

Cherie Burbach

Spring

Spring,
did you hear my call?
I stood out on my back porch and whistled,
like a mother calling her children home to dinner.
My breath left a trail on the cold winter air as I blew.

Spring,
did you see me shiver?
I wore coat upon sweater upon shirt,
mittens to warm my hands
but nothing can warm me like you.

Spring,
did you feel my longing?
I ached for the end of my struggle,
for a sign that what I've waited so long for
would finally come true.

Spring,
reward my patience.
Aid the thaw of my hardened heart,
and as you melt the snow,
let it wash over the sadness I've hid this long winter.

Spring,
offer the robin's song as my refrain
to replace the fear of what I've lost.
Let the sun show me that
years are just numbers
and not the measure of my life.

At The Coffee Shop

At the coffee shop
    she waits

        a cup of chai
        a newspaper
        sympathetic nods from the guy behind the counter
        hungry glances from an old man across the room.

She sips her tea
    and waits

        will he be funny? sweet? charming?
        will he make her laugh and listen to what she has to say?

As the door opens
    she looks up

        the red-haired boy
        with the handsome smile
        nervously greets her
        hurries to order coffee

        and something about him
        makes her smile.

Worth the wait.

Cherie Burbach

The Difference Now

The difference now
      is when pushed
      I push back.

The difference now
      is when I'm hurt
      I'll cry
      openly
      unashamed.

      Why should I hide it?
      Or pretend that I don't care?
      You know you hurt me.
      My pretending only helped you, not me.

The difference now
      is that I'll fight for the life
      I want to live
      and not the one
      you think I should live.

The difference now
      is that I make the definitions
      and throw yours away.

The difference now
      is when I walk in a room
      and you guiltily look at each other
      and stop talking
      I'll wonder who you'll blame
      for the problems in your life
                after I move on.
The difference now

is when you're laughing
behind my back

I realize I must be ahead of you
    and I'll keep going.

Cherie Burbach

Tell Me Again

Have you told me you love me?
Tell me again.
Have you told me you care
      that you'll stay by my side
      that you'll hold me forever?

Tell me again.
And again.

Tell my heart
      and my soul
tell every thought and intention
      every memory, emotion
tell all the worries and doubts
      again and again
      it's me you love. Me.

Tell your old lovers
      your admirers
      your ex-girlfriends
      and the widow that lives next door.
Tell them all, make it known.
Again and again and again.

Shout it from the rooftops
      whisper it in the wind
      write it in a letter
      share it with your touch
      fill up every space with the knowledge
          you love me.

And then tell me again.

This Man I Love

This man I love
with soft caress
his gentle touch
his smile, the best.

This man I love
with kindest heart
respects my words
adores my art.

This man I love
who shares my faith
who prays with me,
accepts His grace.

This man I love
who sees in me
a tender heart,
sincerity.

This man I love
who loves me too
gave me his name,
a life anew.

This man I love
who changed my life
my husband now,
and I, his wife.

Cherie Burbach

Sweet Friend

My friend
> you came to me
> on a bright September day.

My friend
> you promised me
> that love would come my way.

Dear friend
> you told me that
> you'd always, always, stay.

Sweet friend
> your promise kept
> that love did come my way.

Dear friend
> you stole my heart
> when you said goodbye that day.

Bouquet Wrapped With Trust

How did I get here?
This new girl
      living in a new place
      with a new name.
How did it happen?
      When fate took my hand
      and handed me a bouquet
      wrapped with trust
      I had no choice
      but to take it
      the flowers were beautiful
      I reveled in their color
      their simplicity
      not fussy
      not foreign
      simple, graceful.

Cherie Burbach

I took them inside
    put them in a vase
    taking one flower for
        beside the bed
    one for the bathroom
        so I can see it while I brush my teeth
    one in my car
        my handbag
        my desk at work
        until these stems
        were everywhere
        in my house
        and my life
        until I became used to their sight
        uncomplicated and clean
        until I knew
        their sweet scent

        until I could tell the difference
        they made in my life.

No Power Here

You lean to the woman next to you
as I walk in the room
and without manners or decency
ask who I think I am.

You look me up and down
disapproving of my dress
and just for good measure
spread some gossip you have heard.

You sneer as I search the room
for a friend.
So happy you are that
I am alone right now.

But what you don't know
is that woman sitting next to you?
She thinks your cattiness
has no place at this gathering.

Look around, foolish woman!
Do you see that
your nastiness isn't welcome?
Do you realize how out of place you are?

Because this is *my* life
you're in.
Your disapproval
has no power here.

Cherie Burbach

Finite

You wasted your breath
so finite in this life
whispering lies about me.

You felt the satisfaction
in my hurt
at your betrayal.

You spent your words
so finite in our years
speaking hatred about me.

You smiled every time
you heard me
suffer with sadness.

You prayed many prayers
asking God
to bring me down.

You spent these finite moments
pushing me away
while I tried to love you.

I spent them with tears, wondering why,
until God lifted the cloak of shame
you put upon my shoulders.

And I could live joyfully
these finite years,
while you imagined me done.

Beware the Lion

Some people are like
sunlight and water
nourishing your every dream,
putting a fence
around your creativity
to protect you from
those who would
peck it away.

And when you feel
discouraged
they shower you with
words of encouragement
that become light as air
surrounding you,
lifting you
up and up
and out of the darkness.

Others spit jealousy
and anger your way
resenting your ambition
and pouncing
on your hope
like a hungry lion.

No words of love
will help them.
No encouraging hugs
will buoy them.

Cherie Burbach

They stalk your smile,
waiting for you
to tell them happy thoughts
so they can rip them
from your soul.

Seek out the sunlight
when the lion appears,
allow the living water
to wash away the blood
from the animal's attacks.

Clean the wounds
in your spirit
by looking toward
the future,
to your dream,
which grows despite
the lion's drooling
after you.

Your Pretty Words

Your pretty words
like cut flowers
so vibrant and lovely

they fill up the
part of my heart
that is empty,

the part you created
when you
walked away.

Bad timing, you said,
it was long ago,
they said

and yet, it's all
I know
of you.

I accepted
your
pretty words,

admired the
lovely bow
of promises

you tied
around them,
but when I looked

Cherie Burbach

beyond them, all
that was left were
your selfish actions

your loud irritations
at my desire
for something real,

where you'd really
care about me
as the person I am,

where you wouldn't
bellow
your displeasure

each time
you couldn't
get your way.

I wish I could pretend
I had years and years with you
like they did.

That I had
good memories
and love from you,

so I could agree
when they would say
you meant well,

but I had nothing
to hold on to,
besides the fact that you left

and when you got
a second chance
you didn't care about me.

I wish
my desire for it to be
different

was enough
to make
your pretty words

believable
and
sweet.

But after a while
even I could see
the pretty words

had wilted,
and there
was nothing else

I could
hold
on to.

Cherie Burbach

In the Blink of an Eye

My grandpa used to say
that he was once a young man
and he blinked
and found he had been married 20 years.

He blinked again,
and was a grandfather.
Before he knew it
an entire family had grown
in different parts of the country
while he became an old man.

When he looked back
at his life
which had gone by too fast
he found nothing
he could regret.

Dear Younger Self

Dear Younger Self
I wish I could
whisper in your ear
all that I've learned
but part of the fun
was finding out things
through my own
personal mistakes.

I'd like to ask you
to do a few things,
like be good to us
take care of you,
every inch,
and honor
our precious soul.

I'd like to comfort you
especially when you're acting
like someone else
just to try and fit in
to become the girl
that people expect.

I'd like to hold my hands
over your soft little ears
and rock you to sleep
so you won't believe
the lies they are telling you.

Cherie Burbach

I wish I could pull you out
of that party, where
you first met him,
just grab you by the hand
and tell you to run
as far and fast as you could.

I wish I could save you
from every heartbreak
and moment of self-doubt
but I can't.

My years have given me
the power to hold
this wisdom and yours
aren't as strong yet.

So I will tell you this,
that the girl you see
in the mirror
really, truly, is beautiful,
inside and out.

Please tuck that thought away
in your heart
so I can retrieve
it later.

Chapter 3:

How Manifold Are His Works

Angel Toughness

Where did you get
the idea
that angels were
chubby man-babies
with scared looks
on their faces
and wings that float
daintily through the air?

Angels are tough.
The kind of tough
that fights for God
and leaves judgement
to Him.

They're the kind of being
devoted wholeheartedly
to their creator

standing firm
observing quietly
until it is time
to carry out
God's will.

Cherie Burbach

They will not start fights
for their own purpose
not even under the pretense
of it being for God,

but instead go to battle
when instructed to
and fight to the finish
standing gloriously
with God in the end.

Angels are tough.
The kind of tough
I want to be.

Gracefully Dancing

The autumn leaves
fall from the maple tree,
like golden tears of joy,

they fall gracefully
dancing all the way down
before landing at my feet,

like a polite child
that says,
"Hello, pleased to meet you."

Layers upon layers shred
as I hold out my hands
trying to catch each leaf,

and I take in the beauty
of brown branches,
standing proudly in the sunlight

and shield my eyes
as the tree says,
"This is me."

Cherie Burbach

Robin's Nest

The robin sings
"Follow me.
I have a secret
to show you."

She leads me
to a doorway,
where above
sits her nest.

"Isn't it beautiful?"
From a distance,
it is the color of mud,
made with sticks and feathers.

Beautiful?
I shake my head.
"You need to look closely,"
she says, giving me a nudge.

I walk slowly towards it
and see eggs inside,
a brilliant color
of blue.

Their oval shape
set perfectly against
the sharp edges
of the nest.

I reach out
to touch them
and prick
my finger

on the edges
of a twig
that is hidden just
beneath the surface.

As I pull back my hand,
the robin says,
"I patterned this nest
after your heart.

See how you've
been hurt,
just trying to
get near it?

That's what happens
to the people
who try and
love you."

I looked at the nest again,
sturdy and strong,
yet yielding to
the winds of change.

The nest, so plain,
it could blend in
with the background
had the robin chose to hide it.

Instead, it sat
proudly over my doorway,
welcoming everyone in
but using

the rough edges
to protect
its priceless contents
from those who would do harm.

"You can get close,"
she told me,
"with care
and gentleness."

I moved closer
enough to feel
the joy of a life
well loved.

The robin
sang her
song
in triumph.

Early Morning Choir

The birds chirp mightily
through the dark morning hours,
urging the sun
out from its hiding place.

They call out
for warmth, guidance,
over their natural world
and perhaps over ours as well.

They remain steadfast
assured each day
that they will see the sun,
never doubtful of its return.

Their hours of early morning work
are rewarded each day,
as the sun slowly warms their bodies,
offers light to guide their flight.

They sing happily
joyful at the rise
of the new day,
offering praise before they begin
the work that must be done.

Cherie Burbach

The Clear Blue Sky

Violent storms pulled me from my dreams today
as the world outside my window
tried to shield its eyes
from Heaven's gentle cleaning.

I watched the dark sky,
felt the flashes of light that shook the ground
and thanked God for a strong faith,
and for people who love me.

Despite the storms outside
I was unaffected.
Through God's blessings
through His grace
I have risen above haters
and turmoil,
I have thrived despite the neglect
of those who should have loved me
unconditionally.

I've learned the source
the only one
of true love.

It is Him.
I feel His love even now,
as storms keep me locked inside.
I know His grace
and wait for clear blue sky.
It will come again.

The Blessing of Genevieve

She comes to me, gingerly,
as if my distress has called out to her,
like a sound only she can hear.

She sits beside me,
placing her head on my knee
and sighs deeply,
as if she can absorb the sadness from my body.

She stays there, content, unmoving,
and soon the dark fears
that weigh upon my soul subside.

I pet her head
feeling her soft fur between my fingers
and she closes her eyes,
knowing that the affection I give her
is for my own benefit.

Cherie Burbach

What Is Prayer?

Why do I pray to you?
You, who put each hair on my head,
who made my blue eyes
and strong spirit.

Why do I tell you
what you surely must already know.
Why confess the sins you've seen,
or tell you about my fears?

Do I beg to you?
Do I ask you
to do something
you weren't planning on doing?

Is prayer a reminder
for you to fulfill
promises I perceived
from you?

Is it separate
from my thoughts and heart,
sent out with emotion
to the only one who'll understand?

Or should prayers be shouted?
Glory! Blessings! As loud and long
as we can to make sure that you know
what it is we're saying.

No.

Prayer is not so you can see me more clearly,
it is how I can see my faults and weaknesses,
and still show my authentic self
to you.

Prayer is not how you know what I desire,
but how I can more freely
see the blessings
from this path you've led me on.

Prayer lets me step out of
our world of time and space
and into your world, our future home,
when we close our eyes and speak with you.

Prayer is our answer
to the questions we have
before we even know
what we would ask.

Cherie Burbach

Free Pass

I awake to a dark sky
lighter than night
but subdued and grey,
hiding the sun
and possibility for the day.

Ambitions get washed away,
but the rain and thunder
makes me pause enough
to appreciate that this too
is a gift.

This day
is a free pass
to escape
the driving
pace of an ordinary day.

The lighting cracks
the ground,
shakes the house,
reminds me of the One
who is truly in control.

The leaves hold out
their tiny hands
like children,
reaching out to God,
arms extended,

eyes closed,
with smiles that show
their delight
in feeling the rain
upon their faces.

Cherie Burbach

Hope

Hovering
Over
Positive
Expectations

Afternoon Cinema

We entered a room
with no doors or windows,
open to the world and our feelings,

open to the anger we felt,
at having our failures
displayed for all to see.

They played out before us,
and we watched,
rapt with attention,

like people with free tickets
to an afternoon cinema,
munching on our popcorn

entertained at the mistakes of others
but shocked
when our own came up on screen.

So when the showing was over,
we sat, disgusted and amazed
with each other.

How alike we were!
How similar
our regrets and shame.

And all we could do was nod,
and say to each other,
"I understand you."

Cherie Burbach

The Smile

The smile,
so brief and sincere
invites me to share my own,

not just with
this stranger
but with someone else.

Another,
like me,
who doubts themselves.

Just when I wonder
how I'll find
that person

how I'll know
that they're in need
of kindness

a voice reminds me
to be
kind to all

that God's work
will be done
by God.

Cardinal

Red feathers stand out defiantly
against snow heavy branches.
He sits boldly,
refusing to hide
while she perches near him
quietly but strong.
As danger approaches,
he releases a sound,
sharp and searing,
a proclamation
that lets the world know
he is here
and he may move about
to protect himself
but he will not leave.
He is here to guard over her,
and the little ones hidden away.
He is here to
draw oohs and ahhs
as a handmade creation by God.
He might face danger,
and the cruelness of winter,
but he will raise his voice
to celebrate the joy of life
and to those who find him
irritating, too brash, and lacking grace
he will simply fly
to a higher branch
and continue his
own personal song.

Cherie Burbach

A Little Slice of Heaven

Genevieve
looks at me
hopefully.

Will you
take a nap
now?

Time
to
snuggle?

I have things to do
and as
time passes

I do more
and accomplish
less.

Genevieve sleeps
at my feet
snoring loudly

to drown out
the tapping
of the keyboard

and every once in a while
I look down at her
and wonder

what dreams
curly headed dogs
savor at their master's feet.

Genevieve
loses patience,
jumps up

and taps my leg
with her paw,
reminding me

that a person who sits
before a blank screen
is a statue, not a writer,

and finally,
I indulge
her.

She runs down the hall,
jumps up on the bed
and waits for me.

I pull the afghan
my grandma made for me
over us both

and she snuggles up
next to me,
keeping me safe and warm

Cherie Burbach

so I can
close my eyes
and dream.

Her contented sighs
showing me a
little slice of heaven.

Birthday Prayer

If I could blow out
the candles
on my prayer cake

I would wish for
good health
restored family
blessings in every
area of my life.

But prayers aren't wishes.

So instead, I lay open
my truest self
with good intentions
and ask that you forgive
my mistakes
and show me the things
I do right
so I can do them again.

And I thank you
for another year
to use the gifts
you've given me
to love people
as you love me
to show the world
how you've pulled me through
and gave me a life and a purpose.

Cherie Burbach

These thoughts go
into every breath
as I blow out
the candles
on my prayer cake.

My Heart

My heart
held secrets
and shame.

It remained locked away
in a hardened case
with a key
that was lost
somewhere with
my favorite doll
and innocence.

My heart
beat on
to remind me
that God wanted me
in this place
even if no one else did.

It showed me that
one day I'd realize
I was still here
but I was living
as if that key
was going to be found
one day.

My heart
beat out
a rhythm
that told me it wasn't.

Cherie Burbach

It played a tune
I would recognize
as a love song,
and led me on the
path to find you.
Although I didn't
even know
I was wandering.

My heart
beat faster
at the sight of you.

It showed me life
was a real thing
and love was possible
and shame belonged
to the ones that hurt me
and didn't fit in
my beautiful world.

My heart
released
my pain
little by little.

It whispered a secret,
that the best way
to protect it was
to wrap it inside
of my true love's heart.

My heart
beats even stronger now
in rhythm with yours.

Glorious Day

How glorious the day
that begins
with a sleepy kiss
and clings to dreams
too delicious
to abandon
in favor of
opened eyes.

How beautiful the life
infused with hope,
despite scars
so deep they run
all the way through
to the soul.

How amazing the love
that washes away shame,
and blankets fragile hearts
with grace.

How miraculous the gift
of wedded bliss,
shared by two
with souls set on fire
by faith.

How satisfying the night
that ends with a warm embrace
and kisses that share
the day's adventures
with a single breath.

Cherie Burbach

Silent Hummingbird

The blue jay does not
look at the hummingbird
with jealousy, longing for
wings that are so much
different than his own.

It does not raise his head
to the heavens and shout
angrily at God, for not
getting a body that can hover
before a flower,
choosing just the right spot
to drink from.

It does not hope for
the hummingbird's downfall,
or pray that God would
take away the blessings
He has bestowed on
the tiny bird.

Instead it celebrates
its own beauty,
creating an unmistakable,
joyful anthem,
loud and bold,
while the hummingbird
silently flies to
the next flower.

God Speaks

God speaks
in the sunrise
each morning

with the orange light
that says this is
another day,
a new chance.
Enjoy.

God speaks
through the wage of a dog's tail
that shows you
what unconditional love
is all about.

As the storms blow in
God speaks to our fear
showing us a rainbow
so we remember that bad times
don't last forever.

He speaks
through the cry
of a newborn baby
fresh from heaven

whose tears
tell us the place
we'll return
to is good.
So very good.

Cherie Burbach

The Light of the Beloved

Last night
we were driving home from running errands
and I was distracted by the sky.
How can you not stop and appreciate
what Rumi called "the light of the beloved"?

It is truly a work of art,
these clouds and this light and this image.
And yet, here we are,
speeding down the road,
groceries in our car and receipts in our pocket,
the evidence of spending time in the ordinary
moments,
when even then we are blessed with this art show,
unique and free for our eyes...
if only for a moment.

I couldn't stop staring
and pointing
and holding my breath.

How beautiful it is.
See how the light peeks through?
Like God is there,
behind these clouds,
waiting for us to turn our gaze
so he can smile at us through the light.

And what are the clouds
in this holy painting of light and air,
what do they represent
and how do they change
so subtly but so quickly at the same time?

And when the orange dips
lower and lower
so that I find myself
standing on tiptoe to see the last inch of it,
as disappointment and awe makes its way into my heart,
there shines the brightest, most brilliant orange and red,
the final blot of divinity
on this masterpiece that is
now gone forever.

Cherie Burbach

If Dogs Could Talk

I looked into
my doggie's sweet face
and asked her,
"What will you
tell Jesus about me?"

She wagged her tail,
gave me a
wet doggie kiss,
and said
"That you loved me."

I frowned.
"That's it?"

She wagged
her tail again.
"That meant everything!"

The Thing I Don't Appreciate Enough

It is a thing of beauty,
although I've rarely
looked at it
as such.

It was created by you,
and for that reason alone
I should be grateful
for it.

It gives my husband pleasure,
and something to hold onto
during the cold nights
this life sends our way.

It allows me to explore
my creativity,
painting, writing,
all inspiration from you.

It allows me to hold the one
who needs
a friend's embrace
to face another day.

It allows me
to cook and listen
and care
for others.

Cherie Burbach

It holds my soul,
and gives me the secret
to fully embrace
all this world offers.

Poiema

The hummingbird
pauses in front of my window,

hello precious one,
I whisper,
not wanting the sound
of my voice to scare it away.

I'm sorry
there are no flowers for you here, I think,
not wanting to admit
my lacking of gardening skills out loud.

And in the flutter of his wings
I hear
"You are God's poiema"
and realize we all
have our own blessings.

Cherie Burbach

My Angel Dog

Did God give you
the assignment to come to us?
Were you instructed
to gaze at us
with your sweet, dark, eyes
in a way that said,
"Take me home now, please."

Was your role
in my life
to show me,
finally and completely,
what unconditional
love really is?

Did your generous
spirit cause me to
let me guard down,
all the way and at last,
so I can finally
accept God's love
as it was intended?

I call myself
your doggie mommy,
because you are so small,
so in need of care
in this big world,

but we both know
it is you who cares for me
standing guard, protecting me
making sure
I am never alone

living out God's plan
for your life
as I navigate
His plan for mine.

Cherie Burbach

Maple Tree

Going back to the old house
where a new family lives
I drive by, just to see it again.

There is the window I looked out at night
when I couldn't sleep. There is the room
I prayed in when I was afraid.

There is the back stoop,
where I was slapped
again and again.

There is the house next door, where the
sweet couple lived, the ones who became my friends
and gave me a safe place to breathe.

And there is the maple tree, the one I sat beneath
and listened to the leaves tumble down in fall,
the one that made me giggle as the helicopters flew

swirling around my head as I imagined them real,
like a secret force of protectors coming
to take me away and save me from the darkness.

The tree is still there, so much bigger than before.
I sit beneath it again, hoping that the people
who live there now will understand.

I close my eyes and think about
the days that came before.
I don't miss them.

I don't know why I'm here,
and I silently wonder
what drew me back.

And then the tree says, "Because for once
you wanted to feel small and treated like
an innocent little girl. At last, I can give that to you."

Cherie Burbach

The Grace of a New Day

The darkness is easily forgotten
when you rise up and feel the sun
warm you through to your soul.

Stand in the grace of a new day
accepting the gifts you don't yet see
but know are there.

Close your eyes and listen
to the wisdom that was breathed
into your heart before you were born.

You need only open your eyes
to forget what your nightmares
look like.

Where Evening Fades (Tangerine Clouds)

The sun bows low
our silent appreciation
encouraging
an encore

lower and lower
until just a thin sliver remained
casting tangerine light
on the clouds that
moved slowly before us.

We stood silent,
mouths agape
at the sheer beauty
and felt Him here, painting

as we remembered
how often we had
begged Him to show us
a miracle

challenging Him to prove
that He is here
and watching
over us.

Cherie Burbach

As the tangerine clouds
faded to grey
I imagined Him there
nudging me,

saying, how'd you like that one?
as He accepted my appreciation
for the sunset
that painted the sky

with another masterpiece,
one that will fade away
within seconds,
our memory

and that moment of appreciation
the only witness we have
to this
daily miracle.

Hummingbird

The hummingbird
pauses before me
sharing his offer
to carry my prayers
up to heaven.

But I tell him, silly one,
watching you fly
is the miracle that
tells me they are
already there.

Chapter 4:

Gifts of His Grace

My Soul Is From a Different Place

My soul is from a different place
it remembers the day
God placed it gently within this body
that had yet to form.

It tugs at me sometimes
filling me with longing
as it whispers about a place
beyond this world.

It tries to explain the concept of freedom
as I close my eyes, arms wide,
and feel the warmth of the sun
caress my face.

My soul pushes me to connect
while I hesitate,
remember nothing but rejection
as it nudges me toward new friends.

My soul is from a different place,
and one day it will guide me back there,
where He will tell me,
"Welcome home."

Cherie Burbach

Keep Going, Child

A blurry destination
in the distance up ahead.
It whispers to me,
    "Make it known,
        you'll do all that you said."

The faintest hint of roadmap
shows a course that I might take.
A sign ahead says,
    "Ignore the fools that tell you
        mistakes are all you'll make."

Bright lights upon the darkness,
come out to aid the task.
They shine on, urging,
    "Your questions will be answered
        but you'll never know unless you ask."

When exhaustion slows my steps
and adds new lines upon my face,
a gentle breeze will soothe me, saying,
    "Keep going, child, and feel the strength
        of my never-ending grace."

With Every Breath

With every breath
the example of his life
fills my eyes and ears

it is
behind every action
ahead
of every decision
it waits
around every corner
it lights
up the sky
in the morning
and
puts me to bed at night.

It fills my lungs
it guides my life
it weighs in on every decision.

I breathe in
the progress of today
the promise of tomorrow
my life transformed
my greatest lesson.

Cherie Burbach

I breathe out
the self-doubt
the anger
the isolation
the pain.

With every breath,
I live.

You Have Seen Us Through

Dear Lord
Please blow your gentle breath
on the clouds
that have overstayed
their winter welcome.

Ask them to part,
letting the sun reveal
the beauty
that's been hiding
these long cold months.

It's time we
showed our faces.
Let us learn
from the tulips
that will boldly
lead the way,
punching through
the protection of snow
they no longer need.

Let us stand
as courageously
as they,
unafraid of
the harshness of a world
that may not be ready
for our arrival.

Cherie Burbach

Let us be like
the crocus,
practical and diverse,
showing the world
their variety of colors,
their saffron treasure
rare and distinct.

Let us offer
similar gifts,
exquisite and valuable,
adding such unique flavor
to the world
that it cannot be duplicated
by anyone else.

Let us run wild
like the daffodils,
claiming space through
the meadows and woods,
their yellow and orange shades
reminding us of
the life force
in our sun.

Dear Lord,
melt the snow
and erase the coldness
from our hearts.

As the flowers
mark the arrival
of brighter days,
filled with warmth
and beauty,
let us turn our faces
to the sky,
raise our arms, and rejoice,
for you have seen us
through the darkness of winter.

Cherie Burbach

This Night

I searched by it
this night,
> the sign I couldn't help but recognize
> the voice I would hear as The Way.

I clung to it
this night
> the blanket made from failures
> filled with holes, but so warm when wrapped
tightly to my skin.

I ached for it
this night
> the gentle touch under my chin
> turning my head toward the path of grace.

I hoped for it
this night
> the wish I will never have to wish
> the sound of my name, called out by Him.

It's Your Answer

You shout out loud
you cry His name
you demand this answer
it's only right
you're a good person
you think you should get all you've dreamed of.

But when your yelling stops
when you're exhausted, and tearful.

Do you hear it then?
The gentle gnawing of what's right
      the thought of what you should do now.

Do you hear it?
      This answer you've prayed for?

Let go of it all,
      become mute,
      and listen.

It's there
      in your heart,
      where it always was.
It's not your conscience,
      or your mother.
It's your answer.

Cherie Burbach

Do you recognize it?
Can you hear?
Did you really think it'd be the same as your expectation?
It's not your voice, it's His.

Embrace it,
    acknowledge this gift
    that has always been in your heart
    and could now be yours for good
        just like He wanted all along
        just like He told you,
        before you even knew to ask.

And when you did,
    looking up at Him from bended knee
    He responded

more than a feeling
less than a whisper,

it's your answer.

My Prayers

What do you see from way up there
as I bow my head to pray?
Do you see my heart, my struggle,
as I try to find my way?

I follow you, as best I can,
taking in your words and deeds.
I breathe in this life you gave me,
boldly ask for what I need.

Most times, oh Lord, I feel your love,
which brings me a sense of peace.
Other times, I feel your silence,
and my fears become unleashed.

You only, Lord, you are my way
give me hope and love so clear.
Help me remember, once again,
it's your grace that brought me here.

Cherie Burbach

Soar

I begged my spirit to go on ahead
move on from this tired body,
seek out the one who understands
this long journey you've been on.

Feel what it's like to soar.

My spirit traveled beyond
higher than the clouds
deeper than the ocean
farther than my mind or imagination could
comprehend.

When it had reached Him at last,
it felt warmth, peace, and love,
beyond anything this old mind could imagine.

And yet, He said, the time isn't right.
There's more, so much more,
for you to do before you finally come home.

With a wave of His hand,
He showed me my potential.
I felt both humbled, and ashamed.

With His grace, he led me back,
and I could feel the fear, hatred, and cold
grow stronger and stronger
the closer I came to my return.

But unlike before, I understood my purpose.
This time, I wouldn't waste my chance.
Before I entered my body again, He whispered,
"Feel what it's like to soar."

Cherie Burbach

Forever Yours

God,
Make me fearless.

Help me to hold my head up high
even as my naysayers taunt
even as my doubts betray me
even as my enemies throw my past mistakes upon my path.

Make me joyful.

Help me sing your praises and celebrate your goodness
even when I'm forgetful
even when I'm tired and ill-tempered
even when confusion is my constant companion.

Make me patient.

Help me to accept your timing
even if I have to wait forever
even if my life takes a path I didn't expect
even if I'm denied the thing I want most.

Make me grateful.

Help me to see your grace everywhere I turn
even with situations that test me
even with people who have hurt me
even when disappointments have staked a claim upon my heart.

God,
Help me be the person I was meant to be
your follower
forever yours.

Cherie Burbach

Inspired by Grace

Tears falls down my face
at the latest cruel act
that makes me shake my head in confusion,
questioning humanity.

I may stay there all day,
stewing on the carelessness
we hoist upon each other.
I may sit and wonder,
while the heartache in my soul
grows bigger each time
I recall what was done.

But He nudges me.
Interrupts my thoughts,
showing me images,
which turn into reason.
Before I understand it all,
I'm writing.
Words scribbled fast,
inspired by Grace.

When I'm finished,
the words pull me away
further from my heartache
so I see it all
so differently.

They replace my sadness
with hope.
They replace the memory
of my hurt
with knowledge and possibility.

Such is the beauty of God.

Shine

Nasty words surrounded her
like a vicious wind.
They tossed her from side to side,
spit dust in her eyes and pulled her hair,
shaking her confidence and her spirit.

God crooked his finger
made the nasty words dance
down a hole of oblivion.
He whispered to her
in the gentle winds that came
through her window late at night.

He told her, "You are mine,"
and took away the doubts
that cloaked her spirit.
"Shine," He said, "your gifts are
as bright as the stars."

Words like gratitude and joy
surround her now,
like a sunbeam that highlights
the small, tender flowers
that give the sweetest fragrance.

A Cloak of Forgiveness

All I wanted
was an acknowledgement
of what happened
to hear the words "I'm sorry"
once.

That's all that was needed
so we could move on,
and start again.

An apology
not meant to condemn
or even to cause shame,
but to lay down
the blanket of wisdom
on our path
so we could walk freely
without treading on the past
stamping on the pain
that is always there
but lessened with prayer
and God's grace.

Words of apology
could be the barrier over that pain,
allowing us to walk and even run,
feet pounding over it
without it calling up the hurt
and making new cuts
in our mind and heart.

Cherie Burbach

We could have had
a fresh start,
a new path to forge.

But words of apology
would never come.

Instead, more layers were added
to the path of pain,
denials thrown down
depths of rewritten history piled on,
so that the perpetrator wore the mask of the victim.

Each lie, a landmine,
hidden within the path
without logic,
so there was no way to avoid them
as we walked.

Some, kept in a pocket,
tossed in front of me
during times I would least expect,
so I'd be caught off guard,
stumbling to maintain my balance
as explosions erupted around me.

Sometimes, I'd foolishly forge on,
trying to run ahead,
ignoring the fire around me,
pretending my injuries
weren't really there.

Finally, after years of
fighting alone,
I reached up.
And He was there.

He'd been there, all along,
laying down a cloak of forgiveness
that I could cross
and enter a new path.
But I couldn't see Him then,
head bent so low in my own pain,
I never thought to look up.

But when I did,
the cool, soft path He offered
felt good on my feet.
The road ahead of me
was level,
and I could
safely walk
to my destiny
without explosive hatred
slowing me down.

Cherie Burbach

This Is What I Crave

And this is what I crave
these quiet moments
when I can
turn down
the pace of this life
and listen to my Lord.

This is what I long for
these creative moments
when I can
paint the joy
in being a
beautiful,
strong,
grateful
child of God.

This is what I've yearned for
these humble moments
when I can
finally understand
the love God has for me,
now and from the minute
He placed his spirit in my heart.

This is what I've hungered for
these soulful moments
when I can
place pen to paper
and feel my purpose.

Every Jagged Edge

I felt you in my heart
but yet doubted that you
would do good by me.

At each disappointment,
I angrily shouted questions,
asking *why me*.

Sometimes, I would pause,
remain still,
and know that you were there.

I'd see those rare times,
when the big things in my life
were as they should be.

But before long, pain would return,
and along with it,
my questions about you.

My anger paused only long enough
to feel the shame
of my disbelief.

I moved easily
between great love and admiration
to bitterness and guilt.

I thought maybe you *were* great,
as great as I'd heard,
but not for me.

Cherie Burbach

Others would receive your grace,
but I wasn't good enough for it,
or so I believed.

But you persisted,
undaunted by my childish ways,
you refused to leave my heart.

And I matured
in the understanding
of your word.

I could be with you
without hiding
from my imperfection.

My beautiful brokenness
laid open to you,
the one who'd seen it all along.

My arms stretched open,
my face turned up,
surrendering to your love.

My mistakes, fears,
and every jagged edge
caressed by your grace.

Finally, I looked back at the anger and doubt,
and felt the weight of shame
upon my soul.

I thought of the tears
cried out to you,
asking where you were.

I remembered
the pleading, the begging,
for the course of my life to change.

I saw gratitude only after blessings were granted,
and not before,
in anticipation of them.

I bowed my head in apology,
and heard your voice:
Thank you for your honest prayers.

I realized then
there was no need to return to you
because you had never left me.

Called

They called me stupid,
and slow.
My thoughts churned
while they taunted,
and I wished I could
change my introspective ways.

They called me a low life,
a disappointment.
My heart broke with
those words,
and I prayed that
they could see how
wrong they were.

He called me His own,
His child.
My soul burst open
with happiness.
My longing
finally fulfilled.

The Blessing In My Sleepless Night

It used to be
that sleepless nights
would torment me,
heap worry about the coming day
onto my already burdened mind.

I'd toss and turn angrily,
knowing that each minute
I lay awake
would feel like two in the workday.

I'd wonder how to make
it through a day that
hadn't even
arrived yet.

But God has changed that for me.
While the sleepless nights remain,
He urges me from the bed,
invites me to spend time with Him instead.

In prayer,
I thank Him
for the
blessings.

Because sleepless nights
in the middle of a beautiful life
are small gifts,
too plentiful and unrecognized.

Cherie Burbach

Instead
of a night spent
fighting with
covers and worried thoughts,

I find comfort
in a bowed head
and prayers
received.

It's as if God has pulled me from my bed
just to spend this time with Him
when the house is quiet
and filled with His grace.

Beacon

Lord,
I'm surrounded by your blessings,
they spread through the air
and keep me cool from the hot glares
of my enemies.

And yet, I struggle.
I can't see beyond this day,
past this hurt and the
harmful words of
those who choose hate.

I don't have the energy
to look back, again.
I've met my past,
embraced my mistakes
and forgiven those who harmed me,
but my house no longer has room
for yesterday.

So where do I turn?
When my future is uncertain
and my past no longer holds me,
which direction shall I walk?

As I bow my head in despair
I hear the voice,
"Look up."

Cherie Burbach

There is no need to look beyond
what is.
I take the hand He has offered,
close my eyes as I catch my breath,
and feel the light air of blessings
caress my face once again.

He pulls me through,
miles and miles we travel
as I feel the air rush past me.

When I open my eyes,
we are right here,
in the same place as before
but now, I see the beacon
calling me forward.

God's Currency

We worried
and prayed
over money
and bills
but our souls
remained
restless.

We worked
and when
we came home
worked some more
but still,
we felt
unsettled.

We finally
admitted
that it was
all too much
for us,
the worries
and fears
too large
for our
small shoulders.

So we gave it to Him.

Cherie Burbach

And we bowed
our heads again
and thanked Him
for another day,
another chance.

We prayed
over our
sick neighbor,
we asked
for His mercy
for our family
and friends.

And went out
into the world
looking for ways
to spread the love
we'd received
despite our struggles,
to spend
God's currency.

End of Day (Rest, Happy)

I slide into chilly sheets
and slip my arm around you,
your warmth extends out
like a fire heating up my soul
after a long winter's day

My head lays next to yours
so close we are that
our breathing falls in rhythm
and I close eyes
say my nightly prayer
of thanks to God
who is so very good,
and I rest, happy.

Cherie Burbach

Mystery Path

I asked you for the path,
the one that would feel good
on my feet,
the one where I wouldn't
lose my way
where I could move quickly,
making the kind of progress
that made the world
nod its head in approval.

Sometimes, if I
centered myself in stillness,
I could hear you
whispering,
this way…

Other times,
I noticed warning signs
tacked up before me
on tiny pieces of paper
that blended in with the trees
along the way.

But I'd shout out to you,
Can't you give me the map
that shows it all?
Every turn and road and path,
along the terrain of my life?

And you smiled,
saying no, of course not,
that you'd miss me too much
that way.

Cherie Burbach

Faith

Fiercely
Always
Inching
Toward
Hope

His Amazing Love

He listens
as I complain about
the things
He gives me.

He patiently
wipes my tears
as I cry, wondering
if he sends me heartache.

He is there
even when I
accuse Him
of neglect.

He works
through me
as I write and paint
and feel like
I'm wasting my time.

Just when
I think He can't
love me
as he He says,

just when
I start to believe
I'm no one,
so average
that I'm forgettable,

Cherie Burbach

He fills me
with His spirit,
and I gaze
at the mountains
and sky
and stars
and streams

and think,
oh yes,
He loves me
this much.

Be Still and Know

Love's
sweet light
flowing gently
kindly leading.

Cherie Burbach

High Regard

He gave her the assignment,
a tough one
because He cherished her.
Her spirit was strong,
but she'd soon forget that
and ask Him *why*
as tears spilled
from the windows
to her soul.

She'd struggle, feel pain,
and bring the lesson
through for others.

How He valued her!
Holding her tight
even as she wondered
if He really loved her.

Despite her confusion
there were times
when she'd suspected
what her purpose was.

It would sneak up on her
as she made her way
around this life,
doing things she'd deemed
ordinary.

But every once in a while,
she'd feel His nudge,
reminding her of His charge,
telling her about the assignment
and how He would
work through her.

How special she felt!
To be held
in such high regard.

Yet she feared leaving here,
Going back
to where her
story began.

Because she'd forgotten it all,
as she was meant to,
the knowledge that was
siphoned off
as she was pushed through
the confines of time.

Cherie Burbach

He Loves You

He loves you
more than
the stars he created
to guide us

more than
the mountains
that reach for Him
achingly wanting to be close

more than
the birds
that wave to Him
each time they spread their wings.

He loves you
more than
the person you love
most in this world.

Homesick

Maybe the reason I cry at the pain of this world
is that I know what He did for me
to give me
unending peace.

Maybe the reason I feel so tired
at the pettiness and hatred of this world
is that I know what He did for me
to give me
unending love.

Maybe the reason I feel hopeless
at problems that go on and on
is that I know what He did for me
to bring my soul
unending hope.

Maybe the reason I feel empty
at the confusion and wrong in this world
is that I know what He did for me
and I long to go back
to the place I don't remember.

Cherie Burbach

His Child

You've tested me
but not more than He's loved me.

You've weakened my body, perhaps,
    with disease and heartache
    but never,
    not even when I cry out loud
    and ask God why
    will you crush my spirit.

You probably think you've won,
    on the dark days when I'm sad
    and feeling so hopeless.

You probably think I'll turn my back
    on the one who sought me out.
    But you're wrong.

There are times,
    where I'll stumble,
    and even,
    throw myself to the ground in despair.

But in those times,
    the darkest of days,
    I'll still call out His name
    and feel His grace down
    to the root of my soul.

Even at the end,
>	when my tired body is given
>	back to the earth,
>	you might feel victory then,
>	but you'll be wrong.

Because He is the victorious one
>	in the quest for my soul.

As long as there is God
>	my life and heart and mind
>	and all I am
>	belong to Him.

As long as there is God
>	you will not win.

>	And there is always God.

Poiema: New and Selected Poems

About the Author

Cherie Burbach is a poet, freelance writer, and mixed media artist.

She uses book pages, Bible verses, music sheets, and other random things in her art to create a hopeful, faith-filled message.

For more on Cherie, visit her website, cherieburbach.com.

Cherie Burbach

www.ingramcontent.com/pod-product-compliance
Lightning Source LLC
Chambersburg PA
CBHW030431010526
44118CB00011B/581